I0408824

# SHE MEANS BUSINESS

## Breaking Through
## and
## Scaling Up

CINDY COHEN RN, BS BA

Copyright © 2023 Cindy Cohen
All rights reserved.
ISBN: 9798863678498
Imprint: Independently published

All Rights Reserved. No part of this publication may be reproduced in any form or by any means, including scanning, photocopying, or otherwise without prior written permission of the copyright holder.

Disclaimer and Terms of Use: The Author and Publisher has strived to be as accurate and complete as possible in the creation of this book, notwithstanding the fact that he does not warrant or represent at any time that the contents within are accurate due to the rapidly changing nature of the Internet. While all attempts have been made to verify information provided in this publication, the Author and Publisher assumes no responsibility for errors, omissions, or contrary interpretation of the subject matter herein. Any perceived slights of specific persons, peoples, or organizations are unintentional. In practical advice books, like anything else in life, there are no guarantees of income made. Readers are cautioned to reply on their own judgment about their individual circumstances and to act accordingly. This book is not intended for use as a source of legal, business, accounting, or financial advice. All readers are advised to seek the services of competent professionals in legal, business, accounting, and finance fields.

## Bridging the Gap for Women Level Up Residence Program
*This presentation of this story was presented at the 2023 Notre Dame University Idea Center McCloskey New Venture Competition*

I've spent over 40 years of my life helping others find health, but I knew it was time to leave a lasting legacy for the women in my community who were facing entrepreneurial challenges. My own personal journey gave this mission a profound purpose. My mother, a stay-at-home mom with four small children, found herself in a dire situation when my father was suddenly taken from us. Her solution was both inspiring and resourceful—she opened a flower shop, turning our family into a business.

What struck me was the statistic that half of all women who venture into business do so out of necessity, often driven by emergencies like the urgent need for food or financial support for their families.

My life's work became centered on mentoring women entrepreneurs from economically challenged environments. Since its inception in 2017, my initiative faced skepticism from some community organizations, labeling these women as not "real business" owners, unworthy of assistance. But this perception only fueled my determination to elevate these women to the recognition they deserved.

However, the journey wasn't without its challenges. Unseen barriers created by community perceptions continued to plague women entrepreneurs, denying them the recognition they deserved. Many lacked the social capital needed to make connections and advance their businesses, resulting in a staggering failure rate of 26% within the first five years for women-owned businesses, compared to 15% for men—a stark 11% gap.

In June 2018, I embarked on a remarkable journey, driven by a vision to empower and uplift struggling women entrepreneurs. It all began with C2 Your Health Women's Initiative Inc., an organization founded by me, Cindy Cohen, dedicated to bringing hope and respect to women, especially those in low-income neighborhoods and domestic violence environments. At the core of our mission was the Women's Entrepreneur Excellence mentoring certification course, which is the art of our mentoring program.

In April 2023, at the prestigious Notre Dame University Idea Center McCloskey New Venture Competition, I, with my team (Sonya Smith, Wealth In Motion Consulting LLC, Rachel Meredith, Social Kids by Rachel LLC, Mary Lou Stevens, Executive Director Mishawaka Business Association, and our NDU student team Mary Briamonte, Addi Greenbaum, and Kelly Endler) proudly presented Bridging the Gap for Women - Level Up Entrepreneur Residency Program—a new venture aimed to bridge the gap of gender and community bias to transform lives, building upon the foundation laid by our Women's Entrepreneur Excellence mentoring certification course.

And so, the Level Up Entrepreneur Residency Program was born, representing the next level of our established women entrepreneur mentoring initiative. It was a mission to bridge the gap for women who were not being acknowledged as real business owners. I was ready for the challenge!

This program wasn't just a venture; it was a force for good. Women who graduated from our certified course, honing their skills through the Residency Program, would be seen as credible businesswomen. It aimed to reduce barriers to new business creation and development, support industries traditionally excluded, and foster economic development and improved competency.

The solution was clear: build a bridge. A bridge that would match new entrepreneurs with experienced, influential counterparts. This bridge would boost credibility, providing newer entrepreneurs with a competitive edge. Leveraging the "halo effect" that shapes our perceptions of others, this bridge would not only change judgments but also community perceptions, transforming inexperienced entrepreneurs into credible ones.

Our pilot project is set to begin in Michiana communities, starting with females who graduated from the existing women entrepreneur mentoring certification course. Partnerships with local entrepreneur training programs like Ivy Tech College South Bend, South Bend Elkhart Partnership, Saint Mary's College SPARK program and South Bend Entrepreneurship and Adversity Program (SBEAP) are all important for local expansion along with leading entrepreneur support organizations.

The business model was well-thought-out: begin with the certification course, select high-performing, established female entrepreneurs, mentor-mentee matching based on industry, experience, and motivation. Then introduce a membership subscription with annual fees to enhance communication between mentees and mentors.

The most exciting part was knowing that this residency program would create generational change, setting off a ripple effect that would change lives today, tomorrow, and long into the future. One woman's success would positively impact the entire community, bringing hope for a brighter tomorrow.

This is my story, a story of resilience, determination, and the unwavering belief that women entrepreneurs can change the world.

Stay Healthy. Stay Connected. Stay You.
Your mentor and cheerleader,
Cindy Cohen, Founder of C2 Your Health Women's Initiative Inc.

To learn about the Level Up Entrepreneur Residency Program, go to www.bridgethegapforwomen.com

> Supporting women entrepreneurs is one of the most effective tools to revive growth, create jobs, and generate transformational economic impact.

MIT, Solve.org

#BridgeTheGapForWomen

These women entrepreneurs shared their successes with us to be submitted to the Notre Dame University Idea Center McCloskey New Venture Competition with Bridging The Gap for Women - Level Up Entrepreneur Residency Program
*www.bridingthegapforwomen.com*

* * * * *

"Soulful Kitchen is a catering company that launched in 2017. Hope for the Hungry is a non-profit organization that I launched in 2019. Both businesses are rooted in food and serving.

I felt compelled to start a non-profit during the pandemic. I did not know the steps to starting a non-profit organization, so I reached out to C2YHWI women entrepreneurs mentoring. Cindy Cohen sent me the information I needed to get started. We even had a meeting to discuss the process of getting a 501C3.

I am proud to say that both businesses at scaling and the C2YHWI women entrepreneurs mentoring program helped me get to this place.

I was new to the business world and wanted to surround myself around people who knew more than me about business. In starting my business, I did not think anything was holding me back, however my business failed to grow as expected. I was motivated; however, lack of money was stressful, but I thought I had everything I needed. From the C2YHWI women entrepreneurs mentoring program I learned more about business strategies that worked and felt supported from other likeminded people within the mentoring group. As a result of completing the course and certification I gained the support I needed to move forward in my business.

I am looking forward to learning more about the Residency program, I think networking, and connecting with new influential businesspeople is great. So, yes, I am open to it. "

Laquisha Jackson
Owner, Soulful Kitchen LLC
Founder, Hope for the Hungry (501c3)
Graduated from C2YHWI mentoring course & certification (2020)

* * * * *

"As the founder of T&T Ministries, INC (501c3) and the owner of Angels of Integrity Youth & Family Services, LLC, I encountered significant challenges as a small business owner, particularly due to the absence of a robust support system. However, in 2022, my perspective took a remarkable turn when I participated in the C2YHWI mentoring program and earned certification.

This transformative journey empowered me to overcome self-doubt and fear, instilling newfound confidence within me. I'm deeply grateful for the existence of a program tailored to minorities like me. This newfound self-assuredness, combined with valuable resources, has been instrumental in my ability to successfully manage two daycares. Moreover, it has provided me with the courage to run for the school board and embark on a campaign for city council. I wholeheartedly acknowledge that these significant achievements would not have been attainable without the unwavering support of C2 Your Health Women's Initiative.

My positive experience with the program has motivated me to refer three other remarkable women to the mentoring program. I cannot stress enough the importance of continuous guidance, particularly in the ever-evolving landscape of entrepreneurship, where rules, regulations, grants, and laws are in constant flux. I eagerly anticipate the Residency program, which I believe will further enrich my entrepreneurial journey and propel me toward even greater success."

LaQuita Hughes
Founder, T&T Ministries, INC (501(c)3), Owner, Angels of
Integrity Youth & Family Services, LLC, Milestone Academy LLC,
Candidate for Common Council At Large
Graduated from C2YHWI mentoring, course & certification (2022)

• • • • •

"I'm Maria Fleming, the CEO, and Owner of Senior Resource
Network, formerly known as Faith and Family Resource Center, a
business I launched in 2021 with a mission to assist seniors and
disabled citizens in our community, bridging the gap between
financial literacy and technological development.

My journey took a significant turn when I joined the Women's
Entrepreneur Program in February 2021. At that point, my business
was stagnant, and I lacked a clear vision for making a meaningful
impact. Fear held me back, a fear that success might lead to a lack
of love and support. I realized I was inadvertently sabotaging my
business and misallocating resources.

Enrolling in the mentoring program was a pivotal decision. Over
the 12-month course, I underwent a profound transformation. I
shed outdated beliefs that weren't aligned with my purpose, gained
confidence, and developed a solid understanding of running a
sustainable business. My focus shifted, and I started to embody the
role of a "grow giver" rather than a "go-getter," echoing Henry
Ford's wisdom that belief plays a crucial role in our outcomes.

Since graduating, I've rebranded my business as Senior Resource
Network. We serve as a valuable link between the community and
trusted local professionals. When individuals in our community

seek assistance, we can now connect them with the right local experts.

I strongly believe that a Women Entrepreneur Residency Program would be an invaluable continuation of the mentoring program. Pairing us with successful mentors in our respective fields would offer greater access to resources, growth opportunities, and community connections."

Maria Tanksley
Owner, Senior Resource Network
Graduated from C2YHWI mentoring, course & certification (2022)

* * * * *

"Connecting with fellow entrepreneurs, both in group sessions and with my mentor, has been inspiring. The mutual support among women in business is extraordinary. After completing the mentoring course, I knew the value of seeking experienced mentors in my field. These connections have elevated my business.

During the course, I learned the essence of business etiquette and customer-centricity. Planning with the group has also driven business growth, and networking has expanded my relationships and revenue.

The biggest insight for me was the support from this community of women. The courses were phenomenal, and they've propelled me forward with newfound confidence.

Before joining the C2YHWI mentoring program, resources were scarce, especially for women. There were limited women-owned businesses in my community, and I had to dig deeper for help. That's when I found my mentor, Cindy.

As a young lady, I watched my mom and aunt run businesses, which inspired my entrepreneurial journey. My aunt had a rental property, and my mom owned a beauty shop. I started with pop-up shops and eventually opened a storefront called T's Wears. After closing it, I continued selling garments and accessories from my home and truck. Unique Boutique International LLC has thrived for the last three years.

Even the nonprofit H.O.T Hear Our Tears recognizes the importance of mentorship in improving women's businesses in our community. I encourage women to stay the course, learn as much as they can, and find an excellent mentor like Cindy Cohen. Thank you for the opportunity."

Traci Winston Williams
Founder, H.O.T. Hear Our Tears (501c3)
Owner, Unique Boutique International LLC
Graduated with certification from C2YHWI mentoring, course & certification (2020)

● ● ● ● ●

"I started my first business, Vita Harley Originals, in my twenties and even patented a reversible dress. Later, I ventured into designing clothing for exotic dancers, but life took a challenging turn when I became a widow with five children at age 30. I got involved in community activities and discovered my passion for leadership training. Despite still designing clothes, I felt unsupported and decided to shift my focus.

From 1995 to the present, I've been engaged in community work and substitute teaching. My journey with women entrepreneurs began in 2018 when I met Cindy, who was launching C2YHWI. I became part of their mission, helping women and men in our community.

The lack of a support system, fear of success, limited resources, and past traumas held me back from entrepreneurship. The mentoring program provided clarity, tools, and exercises to expand my mindset. It's the key to strategizing and scaling.

During the program, I learned valuable lessons, from marketing and relationship-building to finding mentors and funding. The course boosted my confidence, increased revenue, and expanded my network.

Alongside my fellow entrepreneurs, including Vida Harley, Founder of Women Entrepreneurs Matter and Bridges to Leadership Inc., I embarked on this transformative journey. The most crucial lesson was to brand myself first, then my business. People do business with those they know, like, and trust. Graduating from the program led me to further educational opportunities and community events.

"I'm eager to learn more about the Entrepreneur Residency program as it unfolds."

Vida Harley
Founder, Women Entrepreneurs Matter (501(c)3) and Bridges to Leadership Inc. (501(c)3)
Graduated from C2YHWI mentoring course & certification (2020)

# FORWARD

## The Power of Community, Connections and Commitment

In the world of entrepreneurship, there exists a unique magic—an indomitable spirit that propels individuals to transform dreams into reality, ideas into empires, and challenges into opportunities. It's the spirit of resilience, the spark of innovation, and the unwavering belief that we are, indeed, meant for greatness.

Welcome to "She Means Business," a journey that will ignite your entrepreneurial spirit, fan the flames of your ambition, and provide you with the tools and insights to scale your business to extraordinary heights. Within these pages, you'll discover not just a book but a reservoir of inspiration, knowledge, and unwavering support.

The path to entrepreneurship is a tapestry woven with dreams, persistence, and audacious goals. It's about taking risks, challenging the status quo, and pursuing your passions with unwavering determination. And while the journey may be filled with obstacles, setbacks, and moments of doubt, it's also replete with moments of triumph, growth, and profound self-discovery.

Throughout my own journey and the countless journeys, I've had the privilege to witness, I've learned that entrepreneurship is not just a business—it's a way of life. It's about embracing uncertainty, conquering fears, and daring to dream bigger than ever before. It's about building bridges, breaking barriers, and supporting one another on this incredible voyage.

"She Means Business" is a valuable resource whether you are embarking on a new business venture or seeking clarity on the path ahead. This book serves as a guide for utilizing navigation tools to navigate the often-challenging journey from startup to significant scaling, allowing you to approach this endeavor with greater purpose. This book can be particularly beneficial for businesses that are ready to undertake the journey of hyper-scaling, aiming to expand their operations in a substantial way.

The purpose of this book is to help women entrepreneurs move their business as quickly as possible to the scaling stage, supporting hyper-scaling. As I embarked on the research and concept development of the Level Up Entrepreneur Residency program it became evident that there was ample programming available for brand new startups, but not enough there for the critical stage of scaling. This book aims to bridge that gap and is a response to that need.

As we move forward on this journey together, I invite you to soak in the wisdom within these pages. Allow yourself to dream bigger and reach further than ever before. Your journey as an entrepreneur is not defined by its destination but by the courage and tenacity you display along the way. You can achieve greatness, and your unique path to success is a story waiting to be told.

"She Means Business" is more than just a book; it's a testament to the incredible power that women in business possess. It's a tribute to the audacious dreams that inspire us and the relentless determination that propels us forward. It's a celebration of the journey, the resilience, and the unwavering belief that defines the entrepreneurial spirit.

As you turn the pages of this book, may you find inspiration, guidance, and the unwavering belief that you, too, mean business. May you discover the strength to rise above challenges, the wisdom to make impactful decisions, and the joy that comes from turning your dreams into reality.

Here's to the women who mean business—may your journey be filled with purpose, passion, and the unwavering belief that you can achieve anything you set your mind to. Together, we can create a world where every woman has the opportunity to write her own success story.

With unwavering support and belief in your potential,

Cindy Cohen RN

> **When we help one woman entrepreneur experience success it creates transformative generational change and has an ripple effect today, tomorrow and future generations.**

Feedough.com

"Climbing the ladder of success, she broke through barriers and scaled new heights, proving that in business, determination is the key to her empire's flight."

Cindy Cohen RN, BS BA, Founder, President
C2 Your Health Women's Initiative Inc.

## PREFACE

## Setting Out on the Path of Entrepreneurial Success

In the pages that follow, we delve into a remarkable journey—one of empowerment, inspiration, and transformative growth. "She Means Business" is not just a book; it's a beacon of hope, a wellspring of knowledge, and a testament to the boundless potential of women in the world of entrepreneurship.

Since 2002, I've had the honor of mentoring individuals through my wellness company, facilitating their personal and business development. Throughout this journey, I've had the privilege of witnessing the remarkable determination and resilience that women demonstrate within the challenging landscape of entrepreneurship. Over the years as I've delved further into supporting women facing adversity, particularly those from low-income neighborhoods and domestic violence backgrounds, I've been profoundly moved. This journey has not only enriched my own experiences but also ignited a profound desire to share the insights and knowledge I've acquired along the way.

This book is a collection of articles, blog posts, and research, designed to be a flexible resource for women entrepreneurs at every stage of their journey. It's a culmination of years of learning, mentorship, and the unwavering belief that women can create lasting, impactful businesses.

The purpose of this book is to help women entrepreneurs move their business through the startup stages to scaling up stage. It's a roadmap for navigating the complex terrain of entrepreneurship, from the initial spark of an idea to the exhilarating journey of scaling up.

The significance of this book lies in its response to a critical need — the need for comprehensive support for women entrepreneurs as they move beyond the startup phase. While there is ample programming for brand-new startups, there is often a gap when it comes to scaling existing businesses. "She Means Business" aims to bridge that gap, providing invaluable insights and strategies for hyper-scaling your enterprise.

As you explore these pages, you'll find a wealth of knowledge drawn from my own experiences, research, classes, workshops, and the guidance of business coaches and mentors. Each article is designed to stand on its own, allowing you to dive into the topics that resonate with your current needs and aspirations.

But remember, this journey is not about reaching a final destination; it's about embracing the path, the challenges, and the triumphs along the way. It's about recognizing that entrepreneurship is not just a business venture; it's a way of life, a journey of self-discovery, and a testament to your unwavering belief in your own potential.

Welcome to "She Means Business." Let this book be your companion, your guide, and your source of inspiration as you embark on the extraordinary journey of entrepreneurship. You are capable of greatness, and your journey begins here and now.

# TABLE OF CONTENTS

# 01

## Embracing Your Entrepreneurial Journey

# FULFILLING YOUR BUSINESS POTENTIAL: EMBRACING YOUR AMBITIONS

## "Never underestimate the power of a woman with a dream and the determination to go after it."

### Unknown

These words show the strong spirit of women everywhere who dare to imagine a future they want. Let's explore how dreams can become real success. Your dreams can help your business and make you stronger too. This mix of business and personal growth can make you powerful. Remember, when your business gets better, you also should get better.

Give yourself permission to dream big, envisioning a business that not only succeeds but also leaves a lasting impact on the world. Every great venture starts with embracing a passion and dreaming big. Lock into your passion and embrace those dreams.

To turn your wish to be a business owner into a dream business, dedication to one's business is the cornerstone of transformative success. Become obsessed with your business pouring in 110% commitment. What does this look like? Acknowledge that every milestone and setback is integral to growth, taking the lessons you learned and using that information to move forward. Just as a craftsman selects the finest tools for their trade, an entrepreneur must diligently gather the knowledge, skills, and resources necessary for their journey. This unwavering focus not only sharpens expertise but also fuels resilience, enabling you to navigate the dynamic landscape of business with unwavering determination.

## Build it Big

Building a strong, sustainable, powerful business starts with you formulating a clear picture in your mind of what each next step to success looks like to you, think about how you will get there and how you will know you arrived. It's important to note your entrepreneur journey up to now and moving forward most likely has been and will be a bumpy one, guess what the road ahead will continue to be filled with detours, side trips, potholes, you may even have a broken-down vehicle. If the road gets too rough, pull over but never give up. Keep looking for solutions

## 1. Set Big Goals:

When you started your business, you might have set easy goals. Now it's time to set bigger goals. Think about what your business is about and where you want it to go. Aim for goals that make you excited and maybe a little scared. Don't be afraid to think big. Even if your goals seem crazy now, who knows what could happen? Your possibilities are endless. Goals help guide your dreams and show you where to go.

Spend time thinking about what you want your business to accomplish in the short term and the long term, 3 – 5 years into the future. Set specific, measurable, attainable, relevant, and time-bound (SMART) goals. For instance, you might aim to reach a certain revenue milestone within the first year, expand into new markets within three years, or make a positive impact on a certain number of lives by the end of five years.

Consider the story of Ina Garten's entrepreneurial journey to success. Ina started her business by teaching herself to cook, giving dinner parties in her home to friends, then refining those cooking skills. After a few years she then became the owner of Barefoot Contessa, a 400-square-foot specialty food store. Twenty years later, Barefoot Contessa grew to a 3,000-square-foot emporium where twenty foods and bakers prepared the food then eventually expanded her activities to many best-selling cookbooks, magazine columns, and a popular Food Network television show. [1]

## 2. Surround Yourself with Supportive People

Women tend to see their entrepreneur journey as a solo opportunity, working alone quietly in the background, not asking for help, doing it all by yourself. For many women asking for help has become an exercise in futility. Those around you saying "yes" they will help when what really happens is nothing, then you end up doing all the work yourself anyway. So, you say to yourself, "Why bother, I'll just do it myself." Am I right? Doing it all is an option, however this attitude will slow down or even lock your business up, slowing down your personal and business growth.

The truth is a critical part of your successful business expansion will be your ability to create or join a community of like-minded women. These women connections build confidence, create the opportunity for accountability, provide different perspectives leading to innovation, connect to untapped resources and establish high value relationships. Building an entrepreneurial business is challenging, and having a strong support system can make all the difference.

## 3. Celebrate Your Progress:

As you work on your dreams, remember to celebrate each step. Celebrate the good things, the tough things, and the lessons you

---

[1] https://en.wikipedia.org/wiki/Ina_Garten

learn. Celebrate the progress you make, even if it's small. Celebrate starting your business and the determination that keeps you going.

Celebrating your achievements not only makes you feel good and helps you keep a positive attitude, but it also inspires you to take action and helps to motivate you to move forward whether your entrepreneur journey is easy or hard.

Does it sound funny? Maybe, but research shows that celebrating success is important. Studies by Teresa Amabile from Harvard Business School prove this. Celebrating small achievements helps you reach bigger goals. When people celebrate their small wins, they feel more motivated.[2]

**Becoming a More Powerful Stronger You**

You are your business. Building a stronger business goes hand in hand with building a stronger version of you. If your business is not where you want it to be then you must up your game. Become more than what you already possess. More inspired, more confident, more connected, more skilled, more committed, and more engaged in your community. More of everything that got you here.

Let's explore practical strategies to nurture both aspects:

**1. Invest in Self-Care:**

Running a business is demanding but remember that you are your business's most asset. Without you there is no business. If you get sick, become uncompensated, or unable to work for some reason,

---

[2] Celebrate the Small Stuff. University of Minnesota Extension Center. https://extension.umn.edu/two-you-video-series/celebrate-small-stuff#:~:text=Our%20brains%20are%20wired%20to,every%20day%20enhanced%20their%20motivation.

it's not long before your business is over too. Prioritize self-care to recharge, stay healthy and be at your best. Set aside time for a good night's sleep, relaxation, and recharging, making health food choices, drinking plenty of water, exercise, and activities that bring you joy.

Self-care encompasses physical, emotional, and mental well-being. Practice stress-reducing activities like meditation, yoga, or spending time in nature. Get enough sleep to ensure you wake up refreshed and ready to tackle the day. Pay attention to your emotional needs, and don't hesitate to seek support from friends, family, or professionals when needed. The importance of good self-care can't be overstated.

## 2. Continuously Learn and Grow:

Don't stop learning. Learn more about what you like and about your business. Go to workshops and listen to people who know things you don't. Read books, listen to podcasts, and follow people who inspire you. Learning makes you powerful and helps your business.

When you learn, you become more confident. You can deal with problems better and make smarter choices. Learning also helps you understand new things in your business world.

## 3. Practice Mindfulness:

Mindfulness practices such as meditation and journaling can help you stay centered and focused. They promote self-awareness, helping you align your actions with your aspirations.

In the midst of the fast-paced entrepreneurial journey, it's essential to take moments of stillness. Taking time out each day to refocus, think about the road ahead, and seeking clarity may seem like a waste of time at first. However, as you lean into mindfulness you will gain insight that you did not have before. Mindfulness can help you manage stress, make clearer decisions, and cultivate a positive mindset. Consider starting a daily mindfulness practice, even if it's just for a few minutes each day.

## 4. Take Courageous Actions:

Courage is not the absence of fear; it's acting despite it. Step outside your comfort zone and take bold actions that align with your aspirations. Courage is learned, you are not born with it. Embrace new challenges with a fearless spirit.

I had the chance to hear Cindy Solomon, the author of "The Rules of Woo" and a big promoter of Courageous Leadership, speak at this conference I attended. She really got me thinking about courage. According to her, courage isn't about being fearless, but about pushing forward despite your fears. It's the difference between getting stuck and moving forward. I'll always remember her take on courage. She gave this cool example: being courageous is when you wholeheartedly dive into a proven success system, even when you don't know for sure if it'll work for you. It's like going for it even when there are no guarantees. [3]

As an entrepreneur, you'll for sure encounter situations that require courage. Whether it's pitching your business to potential investors, expanding into a new market, or launching a new product, having the courage to take decisive actions can lead to significant growth opportunities. If being courageous is not one in your list of skill sets,

---

[3] Discover the Power of Courageous Leadership. Cindy Solomon, Leadership Expert
https://cindysolomon.com/

get busy and learn all you can to become more courageous.

## 5. Support Other Women Entrepreneurs:

Supporting other women entrepreneurs not only strengthens the community but also fosters a sense of empowerment and collaboration. As you lift others, you'll find yourself lifted as well.

Build strong business relationships with women entrepreneurs, and women-owned businesses. Develop partnerships with nonprofit organizations that support your brand and align with your mission. Combine marketing efforts through hosting events. Collaborate with women entrepreneurs on projects, share resources, and advocate for each other's businesses. Building a supportive network of women entrepreneurs can lead to new opportunities, partnerships, and a deeper sense of fulfillment in your entrepreneurial journey.

## Unleash Your Power

In this chapter, we've delved into the core of building a strong business and a strong YOU. Embrace your aspirations, no matter how audacious they may seem. Surround yourself with a supportive network, celebrate your achievements, and invest in self-care and continuous learning.

By nurturing yourself, both personally and professionally, you unleash the power within to create a thriving business that reflects your dreams and aspirations. Embrace your uniqueness, and let it shine through your business. Your journey as a woman entrepreneur is filled with endless possibilities.

Remember, you are capable of greatness. Believe in yourself, embrace your aspirations, and let your entrepreneurial spirit soar.

The world is waiting for the unique gifts only you can bring. Unleash the power within, and the possibilities are limitless. The path to a strong business and a strong you begins with a single step—one foot in front of the other.

NOTES:

# Tomecia's Journey

One day I had just had enough of not feeling like I wasn't enough. It was late fall of 2017, and after a series of unfortunate events, I decided I would change everything about life as I knew it. I once heard the saying, if you don't like something, change it. I had never seen anyone change themselves.

I was told we were not powerful enough to change ourselves, but on this ordinary day I prayed, "God I know it's possible, all things are possible to them that believe".

I decided it was possible and I was going to do it. The first thing we changed was my mindset about what it is to be me. I was able to let go of fear of failure, fear of change and fear of success.

I was right, and my life began to improve. What seemed like a short term goal for happiness, soon became a lifelong commitment to creating and evolving as a person. I created a practice to cultivate a state a being that allows me to show up in my life, and in the lives of those I love like never before.

I did not realize I had offered myself a gift, the unconditional love and acceptance I so desperately needed was always available once I chose to love, forgive and accept myself. My passion became accountability to myself. My story has only begun.

**Tomecia Tillman**
**JJT Dispatch & Logistics**
**South Bend, IN**

# BUILDING YOUR SIGNATURE STYLE: CREATING A MEMORABLE AND PROFESSIONAL BRAND IMAGE

*"Style is a way to say who you are*
*without having to speak."*

### Rachel Zoe, American Fashion Designer

In the world of business, every decision you make sends a message, and our wardrobe choices are no exception. As women entrepreneurs, your attire becomes a mirror of your intentions, a tool to shape the impressions and perceptions of those around us.

Whether it's the rolled-up shirt sleeves signaling our readiness to dive into work or the white pantsuit symbolizing our commitment to women's rights, our outfits convey powerful messages. Our clothing choices speak volumes about who you are and what you stand for.

A good place to start is by taking a look into the significance of what your clothing choices, exploring the profound impact of our attire as women entrepreneurs. We'll explore its significance and how it beautifully intertwines with our personal branding. Along the way, we'll illuminate the unconscious biases surrounding women's clothing choices in the workplace. And fear not, for I'll provide you with guidance through the expert lens of an image consultant. Think of this as your empowering and inspiring personal branding adventure. Think of it as your personal branding journey, with a sprinkle of inspiration.

## The Language of Attire: Decoding What Your Outfit Says

Research has shown that what you wear sends non-verbal cues and social signals serving as a visual representation of our identity without saying a word.

It has the power to influence how others perceive us in various aspects, from the level of power and influence you exert to how smart you are perceived to be, and even how much you earn. Every element of your outfit, from the colors and patterns to the accessories and grooming create the crucial first impression, making it essential for women entrepreneurs to be mindful of the messages they convey through their attire.

As a woman entrepreneur, you have a unique opportunity to understand and master this language of attire. It's your chance to authentically express yourself and align your outward appearance with your inner aspirations and professional goals. Your wardrobe isn't just a collection of clothes; it's a canvas for showcasing your incredible story, your unwavering values, and your unparalleled expertise.

Picture this: with each outfit, you leave a lasting impression on everyone you encounter. By harnessing the power of your clothing choices, you have the ability to shape perceptions, build trust, and reinforce your personal brand. Your journey as an entrepreneur is a force to be reckoned with, and your clothing is the bold statement that tells the world, "I am here, I am unstoppable, and I am making an impact!" So, let's embrace this empowering language of attire and use it to propel you toward the success and influence you deserve on your entrepreneurial journey. You've got this!

**Building Your Personal Brand: The Role of Wardrobe Choices**

Fashion, remarkably, emerges as one of the most potent tools for showcasing your brand. Through a carefully curated appearance, you seize the reins of the initial impression others form when they meet you, effortlessly conveying what sets you apart from the crowd.

When creating your signature style, consider how you want to be perceived by your target audience and stakeholders. Choose clothing that reflects your values, expertise, and the unique qualities that set you apart as a woman entrepreneur.

An example of reflecting your business values is if your brand is centered around sustainability and eco-consciousness, incorporating ethically made and eco-friendly clothing into your wardrobe sends a powerful message about your commitment to these principles.

An example of considering your target audience of investors, corporate executives, and high-level clients. These individuals value conservative professionalism, and a polished appearance. In this case you might choose a tailored, classic business suit in neutral colors, understated accessories, and for shoes, closed toe heals or flats. Pay meticulous attention to grooming, making sure your hair and makeup (if worn) are more on the conservative side. In this scenario, your clothing sends a message of competence, reliability, and readiness to engage in serious business discussions.

As you can see, a strong personal brand not only forges a cohesive and unforgettable image but also nurtures trust and credibility with your audience. When your wardrobe selections seamlessly align with your brand, it transforms into an integral component of your personal branding strategy. This strategic fusion not only helps you distinguish yourself in a competitive business landscape but also leaves an indelible impression on individuals who resonate with your vision and values.

## Unconscious Bias and Dress Codes: Navigating Stereotypes

But wait, there's a challenge. Unfortunately, unconscious bias still lingers when it comes to women's fashion in the workspace. Research has shown that both men and women harbor biases against non-traditional styles or assertive choices. These biases can impact the perception of a woman's competence and authority, influencing how she is viewed in professional settings. So, what's the solution? Embrace your unique style! By doing so, you break free from societal norms and redefine what it means to be a professional woman. Let's create a work environment that values individuality and authenticity.

One powerful way to challenge unconscious bias is by consciously embracing a signature style that authentically reflects your personality and brand identity. By owning your unique fashion choices, you break away from societal norms and redefine what it means to be a professional woman. Embracing diversity in clothing styles allows us to challenge these biases and create a work environment that values individuality and authenticity.

Remember that your signature style is an extension of your personal brand, and it should align with your business message. By thoughtfully selecting attire that communicates your values and expertise, you can enhance your professional presence and make a lasting impression on clients, partners, and colleagues.

## Impactful Examples in Women's Entrepreneurship

Let's draw inspiration from some remarkable women in entrepreneurship who've harnessed the power of personal style branding to their advantage. One shining example is Oprah Winfrey, who, throughout her illustrious career, has curated a signature style that radiates elegance, confidence, and authenticity. With a penchant for bold colors and timeless silhouettes, she effortlessly conveys both authority and approachability. Oprah's style perfectly mirrors her personal brand as a media icon and philanthropist, creating an unforgettable and professional image that resonates with audiences worldwide.

Another source of inspiration is Mari Smith, often hailed as the "Queen of Facebook" in the world of social media marketing. Her influential presence and expertise shine through in her wardrobe choices. Mari's signature branding colors are vibrant turquoise and a touch of bling, are her go-to palette – representing her unique look and feel. In her public appearances, she embodies an upbeat, open, caring, and genuinely helpful persona. This holistic approach is an integral part of her brand. She confessed in an interview that 80% of her wardrobe is a shade of blue!

## Understanding the Dress Code in the US

In upscale, high-powered business settings, the dress code is often more formal and conservative. While each industry and company may have its variations, there are some general guidelines to consider:

1. Tailored Suits: A well-tailored suit in classic colors such as navy, black, or charcoal gray exudes professionalism and authority. Consider investing in high-quality suits that fit your body shape impeccably.

2. Elegant Dresses: For formal business occasions, sophisticated dresses in neutral tones or subtle patterns can be a great choice. consider for knee-length or midi dresses that strike the perfect balance between professionalism and style.

3. Statement Accessories: In high-powered settings, accessories can add a touch of personality to your outfit while remaining tasteful and refined. Invest in quality, timeless pieces such as a classic watch, understated jewelry, and a structured handbag.

4. Professional Footwear: Your choice of shoes is crucial in creating a polished look. Consider closed-toe heels or elegant flats that are comfortable for long hours of networking and meetings.

5. Grooming and Presentation: Attention to grooming and presentation is essential in high-powered settings. Ensure your hair is well-groomed, and makeup, if worn, is subtle and professional.

**Dressing for Success in International Business**

In today's globalized business environment, achieving success often involves establishing connections with international partners, clients, and colleagues. Your personal style can significantly impact the impression you make, whether you are hosting international visitors in the U.S. or traveling abroad for business.

It's crucial to recognize that different cultures have their own specific rules regarding women's attire. Therefore, it's essential to thoroughly research and understand the cultural dress code of the country or region where you'll be conducting business. While formal business attire is generally standard in many international business settings, it's worth noting that certain industries, such as technology and startups, may have a more relaxed dress code.

Additionally, consider the significance of color choices, as some cultures may find certain colors disrespectful or inappropriate. It's essential to acknowledge that dress codes for women often differ from those for men. For instance, in some cultures, modesty is highly valued, and conservative attire with minimal skin exposure, including head coverings, may be preferred. In contrast, in other cultures, a more casual approach may be deemed acceptable.

As evident, dress codes can vary significantly within countries, influenced by factors such as industry, location, and company culture. When engaging in international business, it is advisable to conduct thorough research and respect the local dress code and customs to ensure that you make a positive impression and demonstrate respect for the local culture.

For more guidance go to:

1. Online Research: Check travel websites, blogs, and forums for insights on the dress code and cultural norms of the country you'll be visiting. Websites like Culture Crossing (www.culturecrossing.net) offer valuable information on cultural customs, including dress codes.

2. Embassy Websites: Visit the official websites of the destination country's embassies or consulates for traveler guidance, including details on dress codes and cultural etiquette. These sites are a helpful resource for understanding local customs.

3. Seek Local Advice: If possible, consult with local contacts, colleagues, or business partners who are familiar with the customs and expectations in the region you'll be visiting. Their firsthand insights and recommendations can be invaluable.

By carefully considering these points and utilizing available resources, you can ensure that your personal style is a powerful asset in your international business endeavors, helping you make a lasting and positive impression on a global stage.

## Adapting Your Signature Style

While adhering to the dress code, it's essential to adapt your signature style to these upscale settings. Use your unique flair to express your brand identity while maintaining a sense of professionalism.

1. Colors and Patterns: Consider incorporating your brand colors or elements into your wardrobe subtly. A well-placed color accent or pattern can make your outfit memorable while still being appropriate for the setting.

2. Emphasize Confidence: In high-powered business settings, confidence is key. Choose clothing that makes you feel self-assured and empowered, as this will reflect in your demeanor and interactions.

3. Signature Piece: Consider incorporating a signature piece into your wardrobe. This could be a statement blazer, a distinctive piece of jewelry, or even a signature style of eyewear. Such elements can help create a memorable and cohesive brand image.

4. Stay Authentic: While adapting to the setting, remember to stay true to yourself and your personal brand. Your signature style should reflect your unique identity as a businesswoman, allowing you to stand out while maintaining professionalism.

Your signature style is a powerful tool for women entrepreneurs. By understanding the language of attire, navigating unconscious bias, seeking guidance when needed, and aligning with appropriate attire in high-powered business settings, you can create a wardrobe that empowers you and aligns with your business message. Embrace your signature style, and let it be an instrument for your success as a trailblazing woman entrepreneur.

With a distinctive and memorable style, you can confidently showcase the remarkable entrepreneur within you, leaving a lasting impact on the business world.

○ **NOTES:**

# 02

## Establishing Credibility and Building Trust

## UNLEASHING THOUGHT LEADERSHIP THROUGH CONTENT CREATION

*"Leadership is not about being in control.
It is about empowering others to be their
best selves and achieve greatness."*

*Melinda Gates, Co-founder,
Bill and Melinda Gates Foundation*

Have you ever paused to ponder the essence of leadership? What does it truly mean, and how does it manifest in our lives? Leadership, I believe, comes in two distinct forms: formal and informal.

In my view, formal leadership is the type of leadership that is officially appointed, such as the head of a company or the CEO. Formal leaders possess the authority to make decisions that others are bound to follow. On the other hand, informal leadership is not bound by titles or positions; it's a unique kind of influence. Think of it as those who lead without official titles, like the cool kids in high school or the influential members of exclusive clubs. People gravitate towards them, not out of obligation, but because they are inspired by their charisma and conviction.

But here's the beauty of it all: true leadership transcends titles and control. It goes beyond mere authority. Being a genuine leader means inspiring and supporting others while collectively striving towards a common goal.

Imagine thought leadership as the compass guiding your actions and messages, encouraging others to take action or to reconsider their perspectives on the world. It's about creating content that resonates, that sparks change, and that moves people's hearts and minds.

True leadership thrives in environments where knowledge flows freely, where collaboration is second nature, and where inclusivity is the norm. It's about fostering a culture where every voice is heard, valued, and respected.

So, as you travel on your leadership journey, remember that titles and positions are only a small part of the equation. It's your ability to inspire, support, and lead with authenticity that will set you apart as a true leader. The world is waiting for your unique brand of leadership to make a difference, so go out there and inspire others to join you on this incredible journey of growth and transformation.

To be seen as a thought leader matters because it can help you by:

1. **Setting you apart from the crowd**: Thought leadership is your ticket to standing out in a crowded marketplace. It's the beacon that sets you apart from the crowd, and showcases your unique insights, innovative ideas, and expertise. You become to be seen as "a cut above the rest."

2. **Enhancing your reputation**: It's a reputation booster, elevating your credibility, authority, and trustworthiness. Clients, partners, and investors are naturally drawn to those who are recognized authorities in their field. As the kids say, "It gives you street cred"!

3. **Positions You as an Authority**: Thought leadership firmly plants you in the role of an authority figure. It's the nod that says, "This person knows their stuff." Others will look to you for guidance and insight.

4. **Attracting a Following**: As a thought leader, you'll find people naturally gravitating toward you and your company or organization. Your ideas and expertise become magnets, attracting new customers, and business connections and drawing in a dedicated following eager to learn from you.

5. **Driving Success**: Ultimately, leadership paves the way for success. It opens doors to new opportunities, partnerships, and collaborations. It's the fuel that propels your personal and professional growth.

If you have not already, embrace thought leadership not just as a career choice but as a path to shaping your industry, gaining trust, and achieving remarkable success. Become the thought leader you were meant to be and watch as your influence and impact ripple through your industry and beyond.

Some examples of thought leaders in different fields are:

- Steve Jobs, the co-founder of Apple, who revolutionized the technology industry with his visionary products and marketing campaigns
- Brené Brown, a research professor and author, who popularized the concepts of vulnerability, courage, and authenticity in her books and TED talks
- Elon Musk, the founder of Tesla and SpaceX, who is pushing the boundaries of innovation and exploration in the fields of electric vehicles and space travel
- Oprah Winfrey, a media mogul, and philanthropist, who has inspired millions of people with her stories, interviews, and initiatives

**The Power of Content Creation: Types and Examples**

Content creation is your platform for showcasing your expertise and thought leadership. It's like having your own stage to share your knowledge and ideas.

Content comes in various forms:

- **Blogs and Articles:** Well-crafted blog posts and articles establish you as a thought leader. For instance, Mari Smith, a Facebook Marketing Expert, shares valuable marketing tips across platforms.
- **Podcasts:** Starting a podcast doesn't require a perfect voice; it's about connecting with your audience. You can explore different podcast styles, from interviews to solo shows. For inspiration, check out Marie Forleo's "The Marie Forleo Podcast."
- **Videos and Webinars:** Visual content can be powerful in conveying complex ideas. Simon Sinek's TED Talk, "How Great Leaders Inspire Action," made him a thought leader in leadership and management.
- **Ebooks and Whitepapers:** Dive deep into a topic with ebooks or whitepapers. Mary E. Knippel provides writing tips and guides you to write your book as a driver of business growth.

**Resources and Strategies for Content Creation**

To kickstart your content creation journey:

- **Stay Informed:** Keep up with industry trends, read influential books, and attend conferences. Knowledge is the foundation of thought leadership.
- **Understand Your Audience**: Know your target audience's needs and tailor your content to address their challenges.
- **Be Consistent:** Set a content schedule and stick to it. Consistency builds a strong thought leadership presence.
- **Leverage Different Formats:** Don't limit yourself to one format; embrace written, audio, and visual content. Repurpose your content to reach a wider audience.
- **Engage with Your Audience:** Foster meaningful conversations with your audience through comments,

emails, or social media. Interaction deepens your connection and reinforces your authority.

Becoming a thought leader through content creation requires dedication and passion. Remember, it's about adding value and making a positive impact on your industry. Create content that showcases your insights, and watch your influence and expertise grow, establishing you as the go-to authority in your field.

○ **NOTES:**

# A Quick Guide to Speeding up Content Creation

### 1    Identify your niche

When it comes to creating content, narrow your focus to a few specific subject areas that genuinely interest you. Remember, your content can cover a wide range of topics within your niche, as long as it maintains consistency and clarity throughout. Include entertainment, inspiration, education, and advocacy.

### 2    Keep your focus

To make the most of your day, consider setting a daily time limit for social media usage. Once you've reached that limit, it's advisable to shift your focus away from viewing cat videos or other distractions. Set a timer on your phone or watch to keep you on track.

### 3    Read everything and anything

Nourish your brain with intriguing stimuli to ignite inspiration. Embrace the freedom to read anything and everything that captivates your interest in your niche. Become an expert in your field.

### 4    Organize your time

It's beneficial to maintain high standards for yourself. To ensure consistency in your content creation, consider planning ahead and dedicating focused time to it, just as you would with any other important task.

Chapter: 2 "Unleashing Thought Leadership Through Content Creation"
© 2023 copyright Cindy Cohen
She Means Business

# Sonya's Journey

**The Benefits of Community Recognition "Street Cred"**

When I started my business Wealth in Motion Consulting LLC, I teamed up with Cindy Cohen and we reached out to individuals in the community to discuss some of the services we offered and inquire as to how we could work together for impact.

The majority of the individuals we reached out to did not respond to requests for meetups and those who did show up as a courtesy with little interest for collaboration. After entering the Notre Dame McCloskey through the Idea Center and placing in the Semi-finalist rounds, we received meetings with the same individuals willing to work with us and partner with the ventures previously discussed.

The moral of the story, as an entrepreneur I learned it goes a long way to be recognized as a business and individual by key organizations. This gives instant credibility "street cred" and the following are 9 benefits:

1. Credibility: Being associated with reputable organizations or programs like the Notre Dame McCloskey through the Idea Center can instantly boost your business's credibility. When potential partners or clients see that you've been recognized by respected entities, they are more likely to trust your expertise and commitment.

2. Trust and Confidence: Community recognition helps build trust and confidence among your target audience. People are more likely to engage with, invest in, or collaborate with a business or individual who has received recognition from trusted sources. It signals that you are serious about what you do and that others have validated your efforts.

3. Networking Opportunities: As you've experienced, community recognition can open doors to valuable networking opportunities. When your business is acknowledged by key organizations, it often leads to meetings and collaborations that may have been elusive before. It can facilitate connections with like-minded entrepreneurs, potential clients, and other professionals in your industry.

4. Increased Visibility: Recognition within the community can enhance your visibility, both online and offline. It can lead to media coverage, mentions on social media, and increased word-of-mouth referrals. This heightened visibility can attract new customers, partners, and investors.

5. Access to Resources: Many organizations that offer recognition also provide access to resources, mentorship, and support. Being part of such programs can help you gain access to tools, guidance, and funding that can accelerate your business growth.

6. Validation: Community recognition serves as validation of your business concept and the efforts you've put into it. This validation can be reassuring for you as an entrepreneur and can also reassure potential collaborators or investors.

8. Competitive Advantage: In a crowded marketplace, community recognition can set your business apart from the competition. It can act as a unique selling point and give you a competitive advantage when vying for clients, partnerships, or market share.

9. Brand Building: Being recognized by key organizations can contribute to brand building. It helps establish your business as a reputable and trusted entity in the eyes of your target audience.

In summary, community recognition, often referred to as "street cred," can have a substantial positive impact on your business. It not only enhances your credibility and trustworthiness but also opens doors to opportunities that may have been hard to access otherwise. This recognition can be a valuable asset for entrepreneurs looking to grow and succeed in their respective fields.

**Sonya Smith, EMBA**
**Wealth in Motion Consulting LLC**
**CEO, Cofounder**
**Inspiring Business Institute**
**South Bend, IN**

# THE POWER OF STORYTELLING: CONNECTING WITH YOUR AUDIENCE AS A WOMAN ENTREPRENEUR

*"We all have a story.*
*The difference is: do you use the story to empower yourself?*
*Or do you use your story to keep yourself a victim?*
*The question itself empowers you to change your life."*

**Sunny Dawn Johnston, Women's World Columnist**

In the vast world of business, storytelling has emerged as a powerful tool that transcends boundaries, resonates with audiences, and creates lasting connections. Who doesn't like a good story? As a woman entrepreneur, your story is an integral part of your brand identity, and it holds the potential to set your business apart from large corporations, making your business unique and relatable.

Storytelling is like a magical blend of art and science. The art lies in its ability to weave a special connection between you and your audience, while the science is in the methods you use to truly engage and connect with your listeners. It's like painting with words to captivate and connect with those who share in your story.

When you are telling your entrepreneur story you are telling two compelling stories: your personal journey as a woman entrepreneur and the tale of how your business came to be. Unveiling these descriptions will not only humanize your brand but also strengthen the bond between you and your audience.

## The Power of Personal Stories: Unveiling the Woman Entrepreneur

As a woman entrepreneur, you are more than just a business

owner; you are the heart and soul of your venture. Embracing and sharing your personal journey can be a transformative experience that connects you with your audience on a deeper level. Many women entrepreneurs make the mistake of leaving their personal stories behind while focusing solely on the narrative of their business. However, by infusing your brand with the essence of who you are, you showcase authenticity and relatability.

## Embrace Vulnerability and Authenticity

Sharing your vulnerabilities, challenges, and triumphs humanizes your brand, making it more approachable and relatable. Don't shy away from discussing the obstacles you faced, the fears you conquered, and the lessons you learned on your entrepreneurial journey. This transparency creates an emotional connection with your audience, as they see a reflection of themselves in your story.

## Highlight Your Passion and Purpose

Explain the driving force behind your entrepreneurial venture. What ignited the spark within you to start this business? By showcasing your passion and purpose, you inspire your audience and make them believe in your mission. Share your "why" with pride, as it is the heartbeat of your brand.

## Show Your Growth and Resilience

Detailing how you evolved and adapted during challenges showcases your resilience. Share how you have grown both personally and professionally, and how these experiences shaped your business philosophy. This evolution highlights your ability to face adversity head-on, instilling confidence in your audience.

## The Business Story: Uniqueness in the Making

Beyond your personal journey, your business story is an essential component that breathes life into your brand. Sharing the tale of how your business came to be is an opportunity to convey its uniqueness, differentiating it from large corporations that lack the personal touch.

**1. Unveil the Inspiration Behind the Idea:** Every business has a story of inception. Share the eureka moment when the idea for your business struck you. What problem were you trying to solve? What inspired you to take action and turn your vision into reality? By recounting this moment, you create an emotional connection with your audience, who may have experienced similar moments of inspiration.

**2. Highlight the Value Proposition:** What sets your business apart from others? Identify the unique selling points that distinguish your brand. Whether it's exceptional customer service, a personalized approach, or sustainable practices, showcasing your business's distinctiveness captures the attention of your audience.

**3. Relive Milestones and Achievements:** Take your audience on a journey through the significant milestones and achievements of your business. Celebrate growth and success and recognize the individuals who played a vital role in your entrepreneurial journey. This narrative fosters a sense of community and gratitude within your audience.

**4. Customer Success Stories:** Incorporate the stories of satisfied customers who have benefitted from your products or services. Sharing positive experiences and outcomes humanizes your brand and provides social proof of your business's efficacy.

## Leveraging Storytelling: Connecting with Your Audience

Now that we have explored the power of storytelling, let's discuss how to effectively leverage it to connect with your audience:

### ✓ Utilize Multiple Channels

Share your stories across various platforms, including your website, social media, blog, and marketing materials. Consistency in storytelling reinforces your brand's identity and message.

### ✓ Engage in Authentic Conversations

Interact with your audience, responding to comments, messages, and inquiries genuinely and promptly. This fosters a sense of community and builds trust.

### ✓ Incorporate Visual Storytelling

Utilize images, videos, and graphics to enhance your storytelling. Visual content is captivating and can evoke strong emotions, further connecting your audience to your brand.

### ✓ Create Compelling Content

Craft engaging and well-structured content that captivates your audience from the beginning. Use storytelling techniques such as anecdotes, metaphors, and suspense to keep your audience invested.

### ✓ Stay True to Your Brand Identity

Ensure that your stories align with your brand's values, mission, and image. Consistency in storytelling reinforces your brand identity and builds recognition.

## Creating a Lasting Connection

As a woman entrepreneur, your personal journey and business story are your most important tools in your toolbox for creating a lasting connection with your audience. Embrace vulnerability, showcase your passion, and share your unique perspective. By blending your personal journey and the tale of your business, you create a powerful narrative that resonates with your audience.

In this journey of storytelling, remember that the essence of who you are infuses your brand with authenticity, making it unforgettable and distinct. As you continue to share your stories with the world, your business will flourish, and your audience will become more than customers; they will become loyal advocates of your brand. Embrace the art of storytelling and witness the profound impact it has on your entrepreneurial journey.

○ **NOTES:**

# 03

## Scaling Your Business for Growth

## SCALING UP - EMBRACING THE CEO ROLE

*"The journey to becoming a CEO is not about climbing a ladder; it's about forging your path and leading with purpose."*

### Ginni Rometty, Former Chairwoman and CEO of IBM

Embarking on the exhilarating journey of becoming a CEO, I've come to realize that it's not merely about climbing a ladder to the top; it's about carving your own path, guided by a resolute sense of purpose and unwavering determination. As Ginni Rometty, the former Chairwoman and CEO of IBM, wisely put it, "The journey to becoming a CEO is not about climbing a ladder; it's about forging your path and leading with purpose." In the pages ahead, we'll delve into the transformative experience of transitioning from a startup to a scale-up, uncovering the qualities, strategies, and moments that define this thrilling expedition. So, fasten your seatbelts, because we're about to embark on a journey filled with insights, inspiration, and the keys to unlocking your true potential as a CEO.

According to Growth Institute's insightful statistics on their Scale Impact and Reduce Impact[4] blog, the entrepreneurial landscape can be a challenging terrain to navigate. Shockingly, only half of startups manage to endure their initial five years, and a mere one in every 200 ventures successfully transition into the illustrious realm of scale-ups. These numbers paint a vivid picture - exponential growth isn't a path that all can tread. They serve as a global reminder of the selected few who truly elevate their businesses to the next level. However, it's precisely this exceptional journey we're here to explore and decode - the journey of hyper-scaling. So, while these statistics might appear daunting, they also

---

[4] Verne Harnish. Will Your Startup Ever Scale Up? What you need to know. Growth Institute Scale Impact and Reduce Impact. https://blog.growthinstitute.com/scale-up-blueprint/startup-to-scaleup?fbclid=IwAR124o66NGe46BLBflKE7PNXmlhvCm_oeB6cov8GBQqb6kBU-a4bO_uU7TU

underscore the remarkable potential that awaits those who dare to embark on the hyper-scaling adventure.

With this understanding firmly in place, let's now shift our focus to a concept that's vital in today's dynamic business landscape – hyper-scaling. This isn't your typical journey of gradual growth; it's a thrilling leap into the future. Picture it as a rocket launch, propelling you beyond the confines of ordinary success. Hyper-scalers aren't content with merely climbing the ladder; they are trailblazers who rewrite the rules of the game. In the pages that follow, we'll unravel the mysteries of hyper-scaling, discovering how these industry titans outperform their peers, remain unshaken during downturns, and maintain a strong financial footing. These pioneers set the bar high for corporate performance and make audacious moves without hesitation. So, as we delve into this exciting realm of hyper-scaling, be prepared to be inspired and empowered to push your own boundaries.

## Hyper-scaling what is it?

What's that all about, you ask? Well, hyper-scalers are the trailblazers of the business world. They outshine their peers, weather storms with resilience, and always keep their pockets full. These champions of corporate performance aren't afraid to make bold moves that set them apart. As you read on, you'll discover the qualities and factors that make hyper-scaling such a game-changer.

## Benefits of Hyper-scaling

Picture this - soaring above industry standards, staying strong when others falter, and building a war chest of resources. These are just a few of the perks hyper-scaling offers. It's like stepping onto a rocket ship that propels you to new heights, and we're about to show you how.

## Effective Way of Working

Hyper-scalers have their own secret sauce when it comes to working efficiently. They are structured for growth, nurture talent, cultivate culture, and have visionary leadership in place. But how can you replicate their success? Well, we've got the answers.

## Startup to Scale-Up

Starting as a humble startup, your primary goal is to find your place in the market. Prove your product's worth, attract paying customers, and build a strong foundation. It's like taking your first steps.

## Scaling Up

Now, here's where the real adventure begins. Scaling up means securing "go-to market fit." It's about creating a scalable commercial model and perfecting every aspect of your business, from branding to pricing to sales channels. Are you ready to take the leap?

## Survival of the Fittest

Did you know that only half of startups survive their first five years, and just one in 200 becomes a scale-up? It's a tough world out there, and premature scaling can be a major pitfall. But fret not; we'll help you navigate these treacherous waters.

**My Journey:** Speaking from experience, I've been where you are. After facing the challenges of a pandemic year, rethinking my health and business C2YH and where I want to go with the C2YHWI nonprofit I am back on track, leading my organization on the path from startup to scale-up. We've crossed the five-year mark and are ready to move into creating partnerships into the market globally.

So, why is this transition so crucial? Here are my reflections on four key experiences that shed light on the journey:

**Embrace an Abundance Mindset**: Say goodbye to the scarcity mindset that may have held you back in the past. Instead, focus on attracting your Champagne clients—the ones who truly value and benefit from your services. Tailor your offerings to cater specifically to their needs and preferences, and watch your business thrive.

**Shift to Overseeing Your Business**: As you prepare to step into the CEO role, it's time to move away from being a day-to-day employee of your company. Dedicate several hours a week to strategizing, improving, and growing your business. Shift your focus to revenue-generating activities that contribute to long-term growth, rather than merely working for the paycheck.

**Believe in Yourself**: Confidence is key as you step into the CEO role. Believe that you are destined for bigger and better things in your entrepreneurial journey. Don't let naysayers or self-doubt hold you back. Release any tendencies for second-guessing and comparing yourself to others and become your own biggest cheerleader.

But it's not just about mindset; it's about upgrading your business functions. Evaluate, streamline, and innovate to drive efficiency and productivity.

Knowing when it's time to step into the CEO role in your small business can be a pivotal decision for your company's growth and success. Here are some signs that indicate it might be the right time to make the leap:

**Business Expansion:** If your small business is experiencing rapid growth and you find yourself juggling multiple responsibilities, it may be time to step into the CEO role. As the leader of your company, you'll have the authority and vision to steer your business through this growth phase effectively.

**Delegating Duties**: If you have built a strong team and are confident in delegating tasks to them, it shows that you have the support structure in place to take on the CEO role. Trusting your team to handle day-to-day operations allows you to focus on strategic decision-making.

**Visionary Leadership**: As the founder of your small business, you have a unique vision for its future. If you find yourself regularly formulating long-term strategies and setting ambitious goals, it's a sign that you are ready to take on the CEO role and drive your business towards success.

**Business Challenges:** If your business is facing complex challenges that require a strong and centralized leadership, stepping into the CEO role can provide the direction and decision-making needed to overcome these obstacles.

**Financial Stability:** A financially stable business with a consistent revenue stream allows you to focus on higher-level responsibilities. If your business is in a strong financial position, it may be the right time to transition to the CEO role.

**Personal Growth:** If you've invested time in your personal and professional development, honing leadership skills, and gaining industry knowledge, it indicates that you are preparing yourself for the CEO role.

**Business coach or mentor:** Seeking a business coach or mentor is a strategic move that can transform your entrepreneurial journey. Don't wait until it's too late to invest in your business's growth and success. Start exploring your options today and find a business coach who aligns with your vision and values. Embrace this transformative partnership and watch your business soar to new heights of achievement and prosperity. Remember, it's never too late to unlock your business's true potential with the guidance of a skilled and supportive business coach.

Remember, stepping into the CEO role is a major decision that requires careful consideration and preparation. Trust your instincts and evaluate the readiness of both you and your business to take on this leadership position. Surround yourself with a supportive team and seek advice from mentors or business advisors to ensure a smooth and successful transition into the CEO role.

Furthermore, as the CEO, it's essential to focus on long-term vision and goal setting. Create a comprehensive business plan that outlines your objectives, strategies, and the steps needed to achieve success. Establish clear performance metrics to track progress and identify areas for continuous improvement.

Additionally, surround yourself with a positive, uplifting supportive team and trusted advisors. Seek guidance and mentorship from experienced entrepreneurs or business professionals who can provide valuable insights and help you navigate the challenges of the CEO role.

Lastly, as you step into the CEO position, remember that growth and learning are continuous processes. Embrace the journey, celebrate your achievements, and remain open to new opportunities. Trust in your abilities and take bold steps to steer your entrepreneurial business towards even greater heights.

It's a big step forward into the CEO role of your entrepreneurial business is a significant milestone that requires determination, self-belief, and a growth-oriented mindset. By adopting an abundance mindset, shifting your focus to strategic oversight, and wholeheartedly believing in your capabilities, you can confidently embrace the CEO role. Upgrade your business functions, develop a comprehensive business plan, and seek support from mentors to pave the way for success. Embrace this transformative journey and watch your business flourish under your visionary leadership. The possibilities are limitless as you step into the CEO role and make your mark in the entrepreneurial world.

*Image H/T David Sym-Smith Founder, CEO Mobility Ventures*

# LaChelle's Journey

We are in the day and age where content creation and business officially go hand in hand. Regardless of your business type, there is almost always a place where social media can enhance your business.

I have done basically every type of content from written, audio, and video content. My favorite kind of content to create is whiteboard videos where I teach with visuals using a whiteboard.

Here are just a couple of ways that creating content has made a difference in my business.

1: It allowed me to grow an email list of 10,000 people.
2. It allowed me to have 6 figure launches.
3, it has allowed me to get invited by conference hosts to speak at international events.

I would highly encourage businesses to learn to determine how social media can support their type of business and use it to grow your company.

**LaChelle Barnett, CEO**
**Pivot Your Brand**
**South Bend, IN**

# UNLOCKING BUSINESS SUCCESS WITH KPIs FOR GROWTH

*"Embrace what you don't know, especially in the beginning, because what you don't know can become your greatest asset. It ensures that you will absolutely be doing things different from everybody else."*

*Sara Blakely, Founder of Spandex*

Entrepreneurship can often feel like embarking on a journey into a realm of uncertainties, much like tackling a complex puzzle. At first glance, the pieces may not seamlessly align, and the path forward may seem unclear. Yet, to advance in this entrepreneurial landscape, it's essential to welcome the unknown. As you pivot, innovate, and transform, you'll gradually discover each piece of the entrepreneurial puzzle, shaping a distinctive approach that weaves together a tapestry setting you apart from the rest. Sara Blakely's words beautifully encapsulate the very essence of this entrepreneurial spirit that has guided you to this point.

As you delve further into the complicated world of business acceleration, you'll come to realize that entrepreneurship is similar to unraveling a complex puzzle. Success in the business world is no longer about stumbling upon a brilliant idea one morning: it's now about precisely charting a path toward extraordinary success. For those of you who have refined your skills and fortified your aspirations, this journey demands not only vision but also the means to bring that vision to life. It's about transitioning from mere dreams to concrete, tangible accomplishments.

Moving forward, you will begin to look at your business in a new light exploring the crucial pieces of the puzzle known as Key

Performance Indicators (KPIs). Just as a puzzle relies on each piece to form the complete picture, KPIs serve as the essential pieces of the puzzle that guide you. They provide the clarity and direction you need as you navigate the complex landscape of entrepreneurship. They are the missing pieces that, when put in place, ensure you are not just following a well-worn path but forging your own unique trail.

As you explore the art and science of KPIs, you will discover how they can become your trusted companions on this puzzle-solving journey. So, as you start on your exciting adventure of business acceleration, piece by piece, you will unveil the extraordinary picture of your success.

**Understanding Key Performance Indicators (KPIs)**

This whole idea of KPIs can seem a bit scary at first but really once you grow to understand them you will fall in love with them. So, what exactly is a Key Performance Indicator, or KPI? In simple terms, KPIs are measurable pieces of the puzzle that help you gauge how well your business is achieving its objectives and goals. Think of them as the vital signs of your business—metrics that reflect its health and performance.

KPIs are not mere metrics; they are more like your compass, helping you track your journey and stay on course. For the empowered woman entrepreneur, KPIs can be evaluated daily, monthly, and quarterly basis to ensure continuous improvement.

These evaluations encompass four critical areas:

**Quantitative Data:** KPIs allow you to delve into the numbers, from sales and revenue to market growth and customer acquisition. They provide a concrete snapshot of your business's performance.

**Confidence Level:** As an entrepreneur, self-assurance is your fuel. KPIs assess your confidence in various facets of your business, including leadership, sales and marketing, creativity, innovation, and digital skills.

**Access to Resources:** A successful entrepreneur doesn't go it alone. KPIs measure your access to vital business development networks and resources, providing insights into your business's potential for growth.

**Future Business Outlook:** Finally, KPIs look to the future. They serve as a crystal ball, offering glimpses into what lies ahead. By regularly surveying your future business outlook, you can make informed decisions and stay ahead of the curve.

### The Importance of KPIs

Think of KPIs as your business's navigational tool, the same as how a compass guides an explorer on their journeys. KPIs serve as your unwavering business partner, ensuring your business stays on the right track to attain its goals. KPIs not only provide focus and accountability but also offer valuable insights into different features of your business. Here's why they are so important:

**Goal Progress:** KPIs track your progress toward goals, be it higher sales, market growth, or improved customer satisfaction.

**Data-Driven Decisions:** KPIs offer insights for informed decision-making, guiding resource allocation and improvement efforts.

**Early Issue Detection:** KPIs act as early warnings, allowing swift corrective actions for emerging problems.

**Objective Alignment:** KPIs keep business activities aligned with overarching goals, ensuring a focus on what truly matters. Every company will have its onset of KPIs however most companies will need to monitor the following whether your own a service of product driven business.

**Factors That Influence KPI Measurement**

The KPIs you measure are determined by several factors, including:

**Business Goals and Objectives:** Your KPIs should align with your company's overarching goals. Consider what you want to achieve in terms of revenue, growth, customer satisfaction, etc.

**Industry and Market:** Different industries have varying KPIs that are considered standard. Understanding industry benchmarks can help you select relevant KPIs.

**Company Size and Stage:** The size of your company and its growth stage can influence which KPIs are most relevant. Startups may focus on different KPIs than established enterprises.

**Specific Business Model:** Your business model, whether it's e-commerce, subscription based, B2B, or B2C, will dictate which KPIs are most meaningful for tracking performance.

**Target Audience:** Knowing your target audience's preferences and behaviors can guide the selection of KPIs related to customer acquisition, retention, and satisfaction.

**Available Data and Resources:** Consider the availability of data and the resources (tools, personnel) you have for collecting and analyzing KPI data.

**Competitive Landscape:** Analyzing what your competitors measure can provide insights into which KPIs are industry-relevant and competitive.

**Regulatory Requirements:** In some industries, compliance with regulations may necessitate tracking specific KPIs related to ethics, safety, or environmental impact.

**Operational Focus:** Depending on your operational priorities (e.g., cost reduction, innovation, customer service), you may emphasize different KPIs.

**Seasonality:** Seasonal fluctuations in your business may influence which KPIs are most important during certain times of the year.

**Long-Term Strategy:** Consider your long-term strategic goals and which KPIs will help you measure progress toward achieving them.

**Customer Feedback:** Listening to customer feedback and understanding their needs can guide the selection of KPIs related to customer experience and satisfaction.

What you choose to measure should be closely tied to your unique business context, objectives, and circumstances. Careful consideration of these factors will help you select the most relevant and effective KPIs for your organization.

## Aligning with Company Goals and Objectives

KPIs aren't just numbers; they are strategic tools that help you align your actions with your company's overarching goals. By monitoring KPIs that are directly linked to your objectives, you ensure that your business efforts are always moving you closer to where you want to be.

In the realm of business acceleration, KPIs are your trusted companions, helping you map out your journey and ensuring you hit milestones with precision. Embrace these metrics, and watch your business soar to new heights, driven by data, insights, and the wisdom of an experienced, growth-minded woman entrepreneur.

**Key Performance Indicator Checklist**

This empowering checklist is your compass on the journey of developing, implementing, and overseeing Key Performance Indicators (KPIs) meticulously tailored to the unique needs and aspirations of your business. Remember, not every business will measure every item on this list; it's about selecting the few that matter most. Your business is a masterpiece of individuality, and you might even find the need to craft additional categories, just as C2 Your Health Women's Initiative Inc. did with their inspiring inclusion of mentoring, community resources utilization, networking participation, and self-confidence metrics alongside their other KPIs for business elevation.

As you embark on this quest, remember the wisdom of embracing a well-rounded collection of KPIs that encompass the kaleidoscope of your enterprise—embracing the financial, operational, customer-centric, and employee-related dimensions. While the areas of utmost importance may differ from one business to another, the guiding stars remain these five timeless categories, which often shine brightly on the path to success for most organizations. So, embrace the uniqueness of your journey, and let these KPIs be your guiding light to illuminate the way toward your business's brightest future.

- ✓ **Financial Performance KPIs:**
  - ○ Revenue Growth: Track growth percentages over specific timeframes.
  - ○ Profit Margin: Monitor gross and net profit margins.

- o Cash Flow: Assess net cash flow from various activities.
- o Average Transaction Value: Analyze average spending per transaction.
- o Return on Assets (ROA): Evaluate the efficiency of asset utilization.

✓ **Operational Efficiency KPIs**:
- o Inventory Turnover: Measure how quickly inventory is sold.
- o Website Traffic and Conversion: Monitor monthly visitor statistics and conversion rates.
- o Employee Productivity: Assess sales and revenue generated per employee.
- o Return on Investment (ROI): Calculate the ROI for marketing campaigns.
- o Response/Resolution Time: Analyze response and resolution times for customer support.

✓ **Customer Satisfaction and Retention KPIs**:
- o Customer Satisfaction Scores: Gather scores through methods like NPS or CSAT.
- o Customer Feedback: Collect customer feedback and comments.
- o Customer Churn Rate: Calculate the percentage of customers lost over a specific period.
- o Client Retention Rate: Measure the percentage of clients retained.
- o Reasons for Attrition: Identify and analyze reasons for client or customer attrition.

✓ **Customer Acquisition and Lifetime Value KPIs:**

- o Customer Acquisition Cost (CAC): Determine the cost to acquire new customers.
- o Customer Lifetime Value (CLTV): Calculate the average revenue generated from a customer.
- o CLTV vs. CAC Comparison: Assess the relationship between customer lifetime value and acquisition cost.
- o Conversion Rate: Monitor the percentage of leads or prospects that convert into paying customers.
- o Marketing ROI: Evaluate ROI for marketing campaigns and channels.

✓ **Employee Performance and Engagement KPIs:**

- o Employee Satisfaction and Engagement Scores: Administer employee satisfaction surveys.
- o Employee Turnover Rate: Calculate the percentage of employees leaving within a specific timeframe.
- o Employee Productivity: Analyze output per labor hour or revenue per employee.
- o Reasons for Employee Turnover: Identify and address reasons for employee departures.
- o Output per Labor Hour: Measure productivity in production or service-based businesses.

By utilizing this checklist and tailoring it to your specific business needs, you can establish a robust KPI framework that empowers you to measure, evaluate, and enhance performance in these critical areas.

## Essential Elements for Crafting Meaningful KPIs

Creating effective Key Performance Indicators (KPIs) for your company involves several essential elements to ensure they are meaningful, measurable, and aligned with your business goals.

## KPI Key Elements (Chart)

| | | | |
|---|---|---|---|
| Clear Objectives | Start by defining clear and specific objectives and goals. | What do you want to achieve with your KPIs? Do they reflect what's important to you? | Make sure your objectives are aligned with your company's mission, vision, and goals. |
| Relevance | Ensure that your KPIs are relevant to your business. | How do they impact your company's performance? | Reflect on the areas that matter the most. |
| Measurability | Must be measurable and quantifiable. | How will you track and monitor? Percentages? Number? | Define how you will measure each KPI |
| Specificity | Must be specific and well-defined. | When will you know you have reached your goals? | S.M.A.R.T. goal format is helpful. |
| Benchmarking | Consider industry benchmarks, historical | How will you know you are successful? | Study industry standard to drive |

| | data. | | performance. |
|---|---|---|---|
| Frequency | Daily, weekly, monthly, or quarterly assessment. | How often should you measure? | Depending on what your goals are will dictate the frequency. |
| Responsibility | Define who is collecting the data. | Who is acting based on the data collected? What change needs to be made? | Generate a report describing problems identified and resolution based on data collected. |
| Review and Evaluation | Assess their effectiveness & relevance. | What adjustments need to be made? | Continue to support your business goals. |

As you've meticulously crafted your KPIs, monitored your business's progress over time, and honed your understanding of what truly drives success in your unique venture, you are on the path to reaping some remarkable rewards.

This journey of KPI development and implementation isn't just a task; it's a transformational process that can redefine the way you approach your business. By selecting the KPIs that reflect your business's progress and monitoring them diligently, you are positioning yourself for a host of benefits. You'll make more informed decisions, embracing data-driven strategies that steer your business towards its goals. Efficiency will become your ally as you identify and eliminate bottlenecks and redundancies. Your team will rally around a shared vision, fueled by the insights your KPIs provide. With an eye on customer satisfaction and retention, you'll build lasting relationships and brand loyalty.

Moreover, it's worth noting that having well-defined KPIs can significantly ease the process of securing financing for your business. Investors and lenders are often more inclined to support ventures that demonstrate a clear understanding of their performance metrics and a commitment to data-driven decision-making. So, my fellow entrepreneur, keep measuring, keep growing, keep reaching for the stars, and watch as the doors to financial opportunities swing open to fuel your business's ascent to even greater heights!

○ **NOTES:**

C2YHWI current Women Entrepreneur Excellence mentoring, course and certification program measures the business success basics that are grounded in the 6 Foundations of Business Success supporting KPI business growth monitoring monthly and quarterly through business performance surveys. You can find this diagram on www.womemoveforward.info

*Diagram Image: 6 Foundations of Business Success ©2023 C2 Your Health Women's Initiative Inc.*

# 04

# Expanding Your Networks and Visibility

# EMPOWER YOUR ENTREPRENEURIAL JOURNEY WITH A STRONG NETWORK

*"Success is not about climbing up the ladder, it's about creating your own ladder, your own journey."*

*Sheryl Sandberg, Chief Operating Officer of Facebook*

In the grand tapestry of entrepreneurship, your success is woven not only with the threads of ambition, innovation, and determination but also with the intricate connections you forge along the way. As Gina Romero, Managing Director, Connect Women, a respected figure in entrepreneurship, rightly states, *"Networking involves not just what you seek but what you contribute—a key element of networking success."*[5] These words underscore the essence of building empowering entrepreneurial networks. So, let's embark on a journey together, one that explores the art and science of networking, unveiling the incredible power it holds to elevate your entrepreneurial aspirations.

## The Power of Entrepreneurial Networks

Unlocking the potential of strategic networks is essential for propelling your career forward. Consider your network a catalyst, enabling you to achieve more and have a more significant impact on your professional journey. It's more than a collection of acquaintances; it's a web of relationships that helps you accomplish your goals, advance your career, and foster your professional growth.

---

[5] Dennison, K. (2021, December 25). Why networking is still important and how to use it to continue striving in your career.
Forbes. https://www.forbes.com/sites/karadennison/2021/12/25/why-networking-is-still-important-and-how-to-use-it-to-continue-striving-in-your-career/

Herminia Ibarra's *"Building Effective Networks, Discussion Guide"* [6] categorizes networks into three types:

1. **Operational:** These are relationships at work to ensure effective task completion.

2. **Personal:** These are connections you choose and enjoy spending informal time with.

3. **Strategic:** Crucial for career and business advancement, these relationships help you envision your future, champion your ideas, and provide necessary information and resources.

**Establishing a Strategic Network**

Establishing a strategic network can be challenging, especially for women navigating male-dominated entrepreneurial spaces, industries, and workplaces. Despite potential biases and obstacles, view these challenges as opportunities to defy stereotypes, break down barriers, and elevate your career or entrepreneurial endeavors by cultivating meaningful connections.

**Creating a Strong Network Foundation**

Building a robust entrepreneurial network is akin to laying the foundation for a house. Just as a solid foundation provides stability and support for a home, a strong network offers the support and stability your business needs to thrive. It's the groundwork for your entrepreneurial journey, ensuring your business stands tall and resilient amid challenges.

---

[6] Ibarra, Herminia. "Building Effective Networks." *VMware Women's Leadership Innovation Lab,* Stanford University, 2021, https://womensleadership.stanford.edu/resources/voice-influence/building-effective-networks. Accessed 12 Oct. 2023.

Here's why a strong network foundation is crucial:

1. **Support and Encouragement**: Entrepreneurship can be lonely; a network of like-minded individuals who understand your challenges provides invaluable emotional support.

2. **Knowledge Sharing**: Networks expose you to knowledge and expertise, helping you learn from others' experiences, avoid pitfalls, and gain industry insights.

3. **Collaboration Opportunities**: Networks offer collaboration, partnership, and co-founding prospects, amplifying your entrepreneurial efforts.

4. **Access to Resources**: Networks connect you with resources like funding, mentors, and talent.

5. **Accountability**: Being part of a network holds you accountable for your goals, keeping you motivated and on track.

**Benefits of Empowering Entrepreneurial Networks**

Empowering networks transcend basics, fostering a culture of growth and support. Key benefits include:

1. **Confidence Boost**: Empowering networks enhance your self-confidence and belief in your entrepreneurial abilities.
2. **Diverse Perspectives**: Access to diverse ideas and perspectives sparks innovation.
3. **Mentorship**: Empowering networks often include experienced entrepreneurs willing to mentor newcomers.
4. **Emotional Resilience**: Your network provides emotional support and practical advice during tough times.
5. **Long-Term Relationships**: Building lasting connections leads to lifelong friendships and professional relationships.

## Examples of Empowering Entrepreneurial Networks

- Entrepreneur Incubators and Accelerators
- Online Communities
- Local Business Associations
- Mastermind Groups
- City Governments
- Align with Nonprofits

Embrace these avenues to enrich and invigorate your network. Each connection and step within these empowering networks will elevate your entrepreneurial journey. Remember, your network empowers you to realize your dreams and make a meaningful impact in entrepreneurship.

## How to Build Your Empowering Network

Ivan Misner, behind BNI, the world's largest business networking organization, emphasizes, "When you meet someone, you are not just meeting them; you are meeting all their friends, too." Building your network requires active engagement and contribution.

Here's a step-by-step guide outline:

1. Define Your Goals

2. Attend Events

3. Online Presence

4. Seek Mentorship

Empowering networks thrive on reciprocity. Offer help, share experiences, and support others.

Constructing a powerful entrepreneurial network demands active engagement, igniting your passion, seizing opportunities, and making connections that fuel your journey towards success.

## How to Know You are Good at It

Assess your proficiency based on how others perceive you. Success in establishing a strong entrepreneurial network is evident when you notice these indicators:

- **A Connector**: Facilitate connections between individuals in your network for mutual benefit.
- **Sought-After Advisor**: People seek your counsel and value your expertise.
- **Positive Impact**: Foster a constructive and cooperative atmosphere within the network.
- **Tangible Outcomes**: Network interactions yield tangible results, such as partnerships or personal development.

Crafting a powerful entrepreneurial network is a journey requiring time, patience, and persistence. Embrace each connection and challenge as an opportunity for growth and empowerment. Believe in your unique contributions to the entrepreneurial landscape, for your success is a collective goal you share. In the words of Herminia Ibarra, *"Build effective networks to enable you to offer more and have more impact."* Armed with dedication and the right mindset, remarkable feats in entrepreneurship await.

# Stacey's Journey

I am Stacey Black, the founder of Michiana Women Rise, a local networking organization with a mission to unite women in business, entrepreneurship, and those passionately pursuing career advancement and dream realization. My collective commitment is to foster mutual empowerment, paving the way for sustained success. The relationships forged in the course of our journey have proven to be both highly influential and profoundly educational. At each event, the community of women thrives through networking, gaining invaluable insights from accomplished businesswomen. While my initial objective was to inspire, it is immensely gratifying to not only elevate fellow women but also contribute to the achievement of goals among the women of Michiana.

**Stacey Oberly Black**
**Michiana Women Rise**
**Elkhart / Goshen, IN**

# MASTERING THE ART OF NETWORKING: BUILDING LASTING CONNECTIONS

*"Networking is a deposit in the bank of your future and in your startup. It won't happen immediately, but if you do it right, you will continue to receive its dividends for years. I, for one, can network with the best of them! You can too."*

### Charlene Walters, Launch Your Inner Entrepreneur

Networking can mean different things to different people. At its core, it's about building connections. You all have personal networks that include family, friends, and business acquaintances – people to for advice, recommendations, and resources. Think about how you find a doctor or share a movie recommendation with friends. This same principle applies when expanding your business connections.

Work has also evolved, with contract-based services, home-based businesses, and less social interaction. Networking may seem awkward, but it doesn't have to be. Mastering a specific skill set is key, but staying authentic is even more crucial.

Networking is a learnable skill available to all. Success depends on applying these skills effectively, which requires knowledge, practice, and continuous effort. It's an ongoing process that builds lasting connections, exchanges information, and fosters trust among your contacts.

### Expanding Your Circle of Influence Through Networking

Networking goes beyond mere contact-building; it's a means of widening your sphere of influence. When you connect with new individuals, you are not only introduced to them but also to their extensive network of 250 people they know. This expansion of your network brings forth fresh business connections, fosters a vibrant networking community, and enhances profitability. A networking community encompasses strategic alliances, collaborative business partnerships, and co-marketing prospects, all designed to boost success for you and others.

You might initially think, "250 people? I don't know that many individuals." However, don't rush to conclusions just yet. Start by asking yourself specific questions and creating a list. According to Ivan Misner, the founder of Business Networking International, the average person has approximately 250 people they could invite to a special event. To put this to the test, consider who you'd invite to your wedding or the grand opening of your new store if those occasions were happening right now.

The following diagram illustrates networking in action, showcasing my personal experiences with significant opportunities that arose from connecting with individuals in someone else's network. In the first instance (1), networking eventually led to becoming an author in a published book, while in the second instance (2), a chain of contacts resulted in two speaking engagements. This diagram underscores the immense value of expanding your network. It emphasizes the notion that it's not just about who you know but also about who they know, who might want to connect with you, and who recognizes your potential, all contributing to the creation of a potent network that elevates your opportunities.

See it looks something like this:

**Example of Networking in Action**

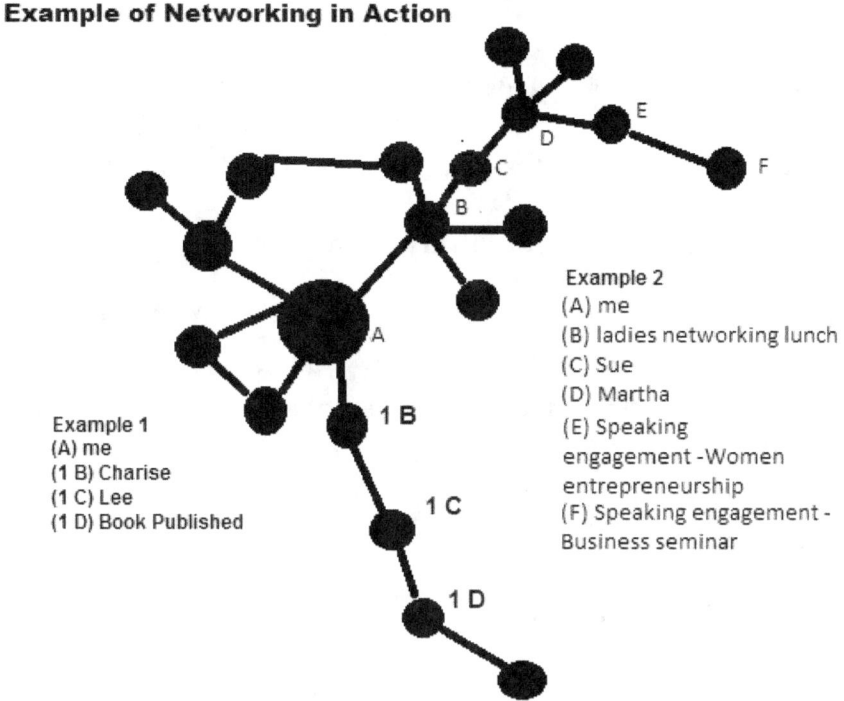

Example 1
(A) me
(1 B) Charise
(1 C) Lee
(1 D) Book Published

Example 2
(A) me
(B) ladies networking lunch
(C) Sue
(D) Martha
(E) Speaking engagement -Women entrepreneurship
(F) Speaking engagement - Business seminar

## Networking Comfortably, Your Way

If large gatherings make you uncomfortable, that's perfectly fine. Start by using your networking skills with one person, perhaps over coffee or in a small business meeting. Then, gradually work your way up to larger events, such as Chamber of Commerce gatherings. The skills remain the same; it's just the application that differs.

People often asked how to develop a large network? You develop a large network by starting where you feel most comfortable, creating one-on-one meetings, then working your way to larger more formal networking organizations and events. A good strategy is to invite someone who is familiar and comfortable to networking attend the event with you as your networking buddy, personal cheerleader, and ice breaker. Wait not loving the networking groups where you live? Join an online networking global group or make your own networking group just the way you like it!

## Networking Opportunities Everywhere

Networking opportunities are virtually limitless. You can network in professional organizations, networking groups, volunteer activities, civic clubs, places of worship, kids' activities, hobbies, recreational activities, and more. In essence, you can network almost anywhere. So, the real question becomes, "Where can't you network?"

## The Significance of Business Etiquette

Business etiquette plays a crucial role in modern networking. It encompasses the principles of good manners and provides valuable guidelines for maintaining professionalism in business settings. In a world where rudeness often goes unchecked, adhering to these etiquette rules is essential. To ensure a positive impression, always be attentive, courteous, and an active listener during meetings and appointments. Maintain focus on the task at hand, refraining from interruptions unless it's an emergency. While some may consider business etiquette old-fashioned, embracing these principles will help you feel confident and at ease in any business situation.

Introductions in a business setting can sometimes feel awkward. Rather than waiting to be introduced by a third party, take the initiative to introduce yourself. When you spot an appropriate break in the conversation, clearly state your name and the name of your company. Follow this with a friendly question to kickstart a meaningful dialogue. Part of business etiquette is the handshake.

## The Importance of Handshakes

A handshake signifies friendship. When meeting someone new, stand up, offer your hand for a handshake, make eye contact, smile, and say their name. The quality of your handshake reflects your confidence and character, leaving a lasting impression. Not shaking hands can be perceived negatively, so don't skip this essential step.

## Four Types of Handshakes:

1. **Hand to Handshake:** The standard handshake extends right hand to right hand with a firm, not overly hard, grasp and shake.

2. **Two-Handed Shake:** Both hands are used, conveying a friendly and warm greeting.

3. **Elbow Handshake:** The right hand is extended for a handshake, with the left hand on the recipient's elbow. This technique is friendly but should be avoided when greeting women.

4. **Dead Fish Handshake:** This handshake is overly limp and unenthusiastic – steer clear of it.

This being said, there are a few situations when handshaking, or touching the person of the opposite sex is not appropriate depending on cultural norms, religious considerations, and personal situations. So, if the person you are meeting does not want to shake your hand, it's not personal, it's something else. Move on.

## Building Rapport: The Key to Successful Networking

Establishing rapport is vital in networking. Think about the last time you met someone and immediately felt a connection – that's rapport. It's mutual trust, connection, and understanding. By building rapport, others will want to spend more time with you and will be more inclined to help and support you. Being a good conversationalist is a crucial part of rapport-building because it helps others feel at ease. To create instant rapport, make eye contact, smile genuinely, and offer a firm and confident handshake. Be supportive, attentive, respectful, and don't shy away from giving sincere compliments.

**Your Networking Toolbox**

Your networking toolbox contains the tools you need to create effective connections. It's essential to have it ready for action at any moment. Your toolbox should include:

- ✓ Elevator Pitch or Business Story memorized
- ✓ Name Badge
- ✓ Business Cards
- ✓ Pen and Notepad
- ✓ Calendar
- ✓ Breath Mints or Gum
- ✓ Water Bottle
- ✓ Small Bag or Folder
- ✓ Information for follow-up
- ✓ Be prepared to put your best foot forward

As an entrepreneur or small business owner, you don't have much of a business if your productivity is low, missing business opportunities due to sick days and spend all your profits on health care. When you are not feeling well it's pretty hard to look and feel your best. It's important to keep your health in check.

**Three Health Habits to Boost Your Performance**

1. **Make Healthy Food Choices:** Consume more fruits, vegetables, fish, and whole grains. Eating right reduces sickness, increases energy, and improves overall health. A proven healthy lifestyle program is One Simple Change, www.wholefood4you.com if eating fruits and vegetables is a challenge for you and your family.

2. **Exercise and Physical Activity:** Regular exercise enhances your quality of life by improving mood, sleep, reducing appetite, and minimizing the risk of disease.

3. **Sleep and Rest:** Quality sleep rejuvenates your mind and body, reduces stress, and helps you process daily information.

## Mastering the Five-Step Formula for Meaningful Conversations

Conversations, much like dance steps, have a formula that makes them easier to navigate. Just as Arthur Murray simplified dance with easy-to-learn techniques, effective conversations rely on a structured approach that becomes more straightforward once you've got the hang of it. Here's your five-step guide:

### Step 1: Define Your Objectives

Before any conversation, set clear goals. Are you aiming to build a friendship, establish a new business connection, seek resources, or ask for assistance? Having a purpose in mind shapes your mindset and boosts your sense of achievement.

### Step 2: Come Prepared

When you are gearing up for a networking event, it's crucial to come prepared not just with your Networking Toolbox, but also with the right mindset. Leave your personal problems at home and the work stress at the job. Show up refreshed and clear-headed, ready to actively listen to others. Remember, attitude is everything in these situations. A positive and receptive attitude can open doors to meaningful connections and opportunities you might have otherwise missed. So, take a deep breath, leave your worries behind, and step into the event with an open heart and a positive outlook. You'll be surprised at the difference it can make in your networking success.

## Step 3: Practice Active Listening

Conversations are a two-way street; it's not just about what you say, but also about what the other person contributes. We've all encountered individuals who only talk about themselves or their business, and it's not the most enjoyable experience. To be heard, you must be willing to listen. Building connections hinges on this fundamental interaction.

## Step 4: Ask Engaging Questions

Keep the conversation flowing by asking thought-provoking questions. Initially, you might prepare a list of questions until spontaneous conversation feels comfortable. Open-ended queries work best, as they encourage detailed responses. Avoid queries that lead to simple "yes" or "no" answers, as they can stifle a discussion.

## Step 5: Read Body Language and Respect Personal Space

Remember that communication involves more than just words—it includes body language. Often, our nonverbal cues convey messages more powerfully than our speech. Pay attention to your posture. For instance, standing or sitting with hunched shoulders and crossed arms signals defensiveness and an unwillingness to engage in productive dialogue. On the other hand, adopting an open and relaxed stance—sitting or standing tall with arms at your sides or in a casual pose—reflects receptivity and an eagerness to communicate, even before you utter a single word.

Furthermore, be attuned to personal space boundaries. In the United States, personal space ranges from 18 inches to 4 feet. Gauge the other person's comfort level by observing their behavior during the conversation. If they start moving away, you might be standing too close. Instead of closing the gap, maintain your position to ensure their comfort.

By mastering these five steps, you'll find that navigating conversations becomes a more natural and enjoyable experience, much like dancing gracefully to a familiar rhythm. Conversations follow a formula.

## Creating Meaningful Conversations

Effective communication during a conversation is vital. Perceptions are formed through verbal and non-verbal cues, as well as visual cues. So, during your conversations, be mindful of:

- Actively listening and staying focused
- Maintaining appropriate personal space
- Maintaining good posture
- Wearing a friendly smile
- Giving genuine compliments

## How to End a Networking Conversation

Ending a conversation can be tricky, but it doesn't have to be awkward. At networking events, everyone is there to make new contacts and reconnect with others, so ending a conversation is expected. To do it gracefully, offer a positive and sincere statement, transition to speaking in the past tense, never cut someone off, provide a reason for your departure, be honest, and remember to shake hands.

## Evaluating Your Networking Experience

After a networking event, it's crucial to evaluate your experience. Ask yourself questions like:

- ✓ How did I present myself?
- ✓ Was I prepared?
- ✓ Did I collect business cards?
- ✓ How was my introduction, handshake, and conversation?
- ✓ Was I authentic, pleasant, friendly, kind, and helpful?

Remember to evaluate your behavior from the other person's point of view. Congratulate yourself on a job well done, and don't forget to follow up with your new connections. Without follow-ups, a networking event is just another social gathering, not a business-building opportunity.

## Never Stop Networking

It's a significant mistake to stop networking. When you disappear from the networking scene, you become invisible. In today's economic climate, this can be detrimental to your business. Always keep your calendar full of face-to-face networking opportunities and continue to engage in networking activities. Networking is a valuable way to exchange ideas, information, talents, and experiences. While it may not yield instant results, it brings long-term value to your business and life. Networking is a skill set that encompasses etiquette, rapport building, handshaking, effective conversation, making connections, listening, and follow-up. Success in networking creates a community of people who can help you expand your business connections, increase profitability, advance your career, and foster lifelong friendships – all while having fun.

## 9 Networking Organizations
## You Might Want to Consider Joining

1. Women Entrepreneur Meetups
2. Mastermind Groups
3. Women In Business Networking
4. Count Me In
5. The Societe
6. The Lean In Network Circles
7. Women Who Start Up
8. Forward Ladies
9. National Black Women's Network

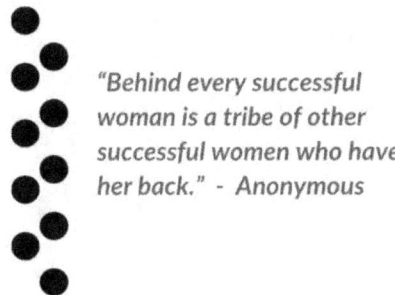

*"Behind every successful woman is a tribe of other successful women who have her back." - Anonymous*

# 05

## Creating Valuable Connections in the Business Community

# Traci's Journey

My role model was my mom. She owned a beauty shop and also my aunt who rented rooms out to people in the community. I owned Tee's Wear in 1994, back then no one was really talking about business mentors /coaches, well not to me, outside of the two very strong ladies that raised me.

When I closed in 1996 to take care of my mom I didn't give up my car and the garage was my business spots, to this day I continue to meet customers to keep the schedule going Cindy and I had conversations: What is the percentage of women-owned businesses? What do the numbers say for minority businesses in the community?

Well, Cindy was intrigued to find these numbers out and to also find these business owners in the community. Partnering with C2 Your Health Women's Initiative Inc. in 2018 was a true game changer in personal and business relationships then in 2019 Covid-19 happened. Just opening up a brick-and-mortar boutique was very interesting. I was shifting with several businesses BMWS & HOUSING LLC, Unique Boutique International LLC, Unique Juice Plus, and a nonprofit organization H.O.T. Hear Our Tears domestic violence awareness. Cindy Cohen is my mentor, Cindy said to me in early 2018 "Get that business plan, get QuickBooks now, get a bookkeeper, update that business plan and wear your buttons ask me about my business,"

Cindy noticed I was an introvert who needed to be bold and embrace what I was offering and helping people with my for-profits and nonprofits.

In the Women Move Forward Initiative, a dynamic collaboration has taken shape, uniting C2YHWI and The Pokagon Fund. Together, they've crafted the Women Entrepreneur Women Move Forward Mentoring Online Community, while also launching the H.O.T Domestic Violence Community Ambassador program. This initiative not only educates our community on how they can contribute but also integrates vital domestic violence support into the mentoring program.

The partnership has been nothing short of remarkable, leading to the discovery of a multitude of talented entrepreneurs within our community. It's with great excitement that Cindy and I came together to form the Women Move Forward Initiative. This initiative is designed to provide much-needed support for women in domestic violence environments, and alongside our thriving entrepreneur mentoring membership community, it paves the way for greater entrepreneurial business resilience on my journey.

As Cindy always says: "I can help you with that or I know someone you should have a meeting with to help your business." Making an impact for all women business entrepreneurs has grown my community. With the team of mentors and coaches and success connections, resources inspiring entrepreneurs my business continues to flourish and grow.

Through engaging in mentor group discussions, attending meetings, and participating in training sessions, I've gained a wealth of knowledge. The experience has been invaluable in my pursuit of scaling my businesses, including Unique Boutique International, LLC, H.O.T Hear Our Tears for domestic violence awareness, and BMWS and Housing, LLC. The guidance and support from our amazing mentors and coaches have been a tremendous source of inspiration and motivation, driving me forward on my journey towards continued success in business.

Traci Winston Williams
Unique Boutique Internationa LLC
H.O.T. Hear Our Tears - Founder
South Bend, IN

## THE POWER OF STRATEGIC SMALL-BUSINESS PARTNERSHIPS AND COLLABORATIONS

*"Alone, you can do so little; together, we can do so much."*

*Helen Keller, American Author, Educator*

Today, we're diving headfirst into the invigorating world of strategic small-business private – nonprofit partnerships, informal and formal strategic alliances, and collaborations. As you learn to navigate the entrepreneur landscape creating business partnerships and collaborations are not just about possibilities; it's about turning those possibilities into realities that will redefine your entrepreneurial journey. Brace yourself for an inspiring adventure filled with opportunities, creative sparks, and the assurance of boundless growth.

**Collaborations / Strategic Alliances**

Collaborating is like when two friends decide to work together on a project for a little while. It's like saying, *"Hey, let's team up and combine our skills to make something cool happen!"* Collaborations are often for a specific task or project, and once it's done, you might go back to doing your own separate things. Collaborations can be formal or informal agreements between individuals, businesses, and organizations. An informal collaboration is sometimes referred to as a strategic alliance.

Here's a short example of a collaboration between two businesses:

Imagine a small local bakery and a nearby coffee shop decide to collaborate for a special promotion. They create a "Morning Delights" package where customers can buy a delicious pastry from the bakery along with a freshly brewed coffee from the coffee shop at a discounted price. Both businesses promote this special offer to their customers, and they share the costs of advertising.

In this collaboration, the bakery and coffee shop are working together for a limited time to offer something extra special to their customers. It helps them attract more customers to their respective shops and encourages people to visit both places, benefiting both businesses in the process.

So, in short, collaborations are like short-term teamwork adventures, while partnerships are like long-term commitments where you work closely together for a common goal, almost like starting a mini business with a friend!

**Partnerships Private**

Partnerships, on the other hand, are a bit more serious, like when you and your best friend decide to start a club together. In a partnership, you are in it for the long run, and you share everything, from the work to the rewards. It's like saying, *"We're a team, and we're committed to making our club the best it can be, together!"* For this there is generally a formal agreement outlining the specific responsibilities of each partner. Partnerships can be between individuals, companies, and non-profit organizations interchangeably. Keep reading to the scoop on partnering with a non-profit organization might be beneficial to your business.

Here is an example of a partnership between two small companies, a small web design agency and a local marketing consultancy joining forces to enhance their service offerings. They refer clients to each other for complementary services, work together on projects, share industry insights and tools, and even cut down on overhead costs by sharing a workspace and administrative staff. This arrangement enables them to provide a more comprehensive range of services to clients while optimizing their operational efficiency and fostering business growth.

## The Nonprofit Partnership

Beyond small-business collaborations, let's delve into the realm of partnering with nonprofits. These alliances hold the potential for profound impact, both socially and economically.

Imagine your small business aligning with a nonprofit dedicated to education. Together, you could create scholarship programs, mentorship initiatives, or even sponsor local schools. This not only helps your community but also reinforces your brand as socially responsible and compassionate.

The partnership between a non-profit organization and a private company is called a private-nonprofit partnership. This partnership is considered a mutually beneficial business partnership or joint venture between a for-profit company non-profit company and nonprofit organization. [7]

Here's a short example of a partnership between a business and a nonprofit organization:

A local restaurant partners with a nonprofit dedicated to addressing food insecurity in their community. The restaurant commits to donating a portion of their daily profits to the nonprofit, and in return, the nonprofit helps promote the restaurant's charitable efforts through their social media channels and events.

---

[7] Private-Nonprofit Partnership Model | The Four Lenses Strategic Framework (4lenses.org)

In this partnership, the restaurant, and the nonprofit work together to address a pressing social issue – food insecurity. The restaurant's financial contribution helps support the nonprofit's mission, and the nonprofit, in turn, raises awareness about the restaurant's commitment to making a positive impact in the community. This collaboration benefits both parties while making a meaningful difference in the lives of those facing food insecurity.

**The Small Business Competitive Advantage**

Ok, let's talk about the incredible advantages that small businesses can gain from B2B partnerships, private-nonprofit collaborations, and strategic alliances. These approaches open up doors to new opportunities and growth like no other. In B2B partnerships, you are essentially teaming up with like-minded businesses to expand your reach, pool resources, and share expertise. It's a win-win, as you both can tap into each other's strengths and customer bases, creating a stronger competitive edge.

Now, private-nonprofit partnerships are all about giving back while growing. By teaming up with a nonprofit, you're not only supporting a worthy cause but also enhancing your corporate social responsibility. These collaborations can create a positive image for your brand and connect you with a broader audience, ultimately boosting your business.

And don't forget strategic alliances. These allow you to join forces with another business to achieve common goals. You can share costs, enter new markets, and innovate together. It's a fantastic way for small businesses to access resources and expertise they might not have on their own.

In essence, these approaches are all about teamwork, and they are goldmines for small businesses looking to thrive in a competitive landscape. So, think about how these partnerships and collaborations can benefit your business and take those steps toward growth and success.

## Benefits of Collaborating A Closer Look

Beyond the immediate advantages, collaborations bring a myriad of additional benefits to your small business journey. Here's a closer look at how these alliances can elevate your entrepreneurial experience:

**1. Expanded Expertise:** Collaborations allow you to tap into the expertise of your partners. You can learn from their experiences, gain new skills, and broaden your knowledge base, ultimately making you a more well-rounded entrepreneur.

**2. Creative Innovation:** The fusion of different perspectives often sparks creative innovation. Collaborations encourage out-of-the-box thinking, leading to fresh ideas, unique products or services, and exciting marketing campaigns.

**3. Risk Mitigation:** Sharing resources and responsibilities with partners can help distribute risks. This can be especially valuable during economic downturns or unexpected challenges, ensuring your business remains resilient.

**4. Diverse Customer Base:** Collaborations introduce your brand to a wider audience. You can connect with your partner's customer base, increasing your reach and potentially gaining long-term customers.

**5. Enhanced Brand Reputation:** Partnering with reputable businesses or nonprofits can enhance your brand's reputation. It reflects positively on your commitment to quality, integrity, and social responsibility.

**6. Cost Efficiency:** Collaborations often lead to cost savings. Shared marketing efforts, resources, and even office space can significantly reduce your operational expenses.

**7. Increased Productivity**: With more hands-on deck, you can accomplish tasks more efficiently. Collaborations free up your time to focus on core business activities and growth strategies.

**8. Emotional Support**: Entrepreneurship can be a lonely journey at times. Collaborative ventures provide emotional support as you navigate challenges together, boosting your resilience and motivation.

**9. Sustainability Initiatives:** Partnerships with environmentally conscious organizations can help you implement sustainable practices within your business, reducing your environmental footprint.

**10. Community Engagement:** Collaborations strengthen your ties to the local community. Engaging in community-driven initiatives can lead to a loyal customer base that appreciates your commitment to local causes.

**Your Collaborative Success Story**

Now, it's time to chart your path to collaborative success. Consider the following:

**1. Identify Your Goals:** What do you hope to achieve through partnerships and collaborations? Increased sales, brand exposure, community engagement, or social impact?

2. **Know Your Value:** Understand what your small business brings to the table. Whether it's a loyal customer base, unique products, or local influence, recognize your strengths.

3. **Seek the Right Partners:** Choose partners who align with your values and goals. Whether it's another small business or a nonprofit, synergy is key.

4. **Craft a Win-Win Strategy:** Develop a strategy that benefits all parties involved. Ensure that the collaboration offers value to both you and your partner.

5. **Promote Your Collaborations:** Share the exciting news with your audience. Leverage social media, email marketing, and local press to maximize visibility.

Remember, the journey of partnerships and collaborations is not just about growth but also about creating a ripple effect of positive change in your community. Embrace the power of collaboration, and together, we'll write the next chapter of your entrepreneurial success story.

**Learning Resources From the Best**

**Blogs and Podcasts:** The journey of partnerships and collaborations is made smoother with knowledge. There's no better way to gain insights and wisdom than by learning from those who've walked the path before us. Here are some outstanding blogs and podcasts to guide you:

**Blogs**

1. "Entrepreneur" – A treasure trove of articles on collaboration and partnership strategies.

2. "Harvard Business Review" – Offers in-depth case studies and expert analysis on successful collaborations.

3. "Small Business Trends" – Focuses on small-business partnerships, with practical tips and success stories.

**Podcasts**

1. "The Collaborative Business Podcast" – Interviews with entrepreneurs who have harnessed the power of collaboration.

2. "Business Wars" – Engaging storytelling of famous business battles, including collaborations.

3. "How I Built This" – Inspirational stories of entrepreneurs and their journey to success, often involving partnerships

As you continue to explore and investigate into the world of collaborations, partnerships and strategic alliances remember that the true magic lies not only in the growth of your business but also in the positive impact you create within your industry and community. Collaborate wisely and let your entrepreneurial spirit shine brightly.

# Nontuthuzelo's Journey

"Mother of comforters" is the meaning of my Xhosa name, "Nontuthuzelo." My surname, Sisale, has Malawian origins, and I epitomize a young, gifted, black female who strives to make a genuine difference in Zimbabwe and the world as a whole.

My quest is to empower minorities, especially young women, by bridging the gender financial literacy gap and improving access to microloans to help this group achieve financial and social freedom.

"Akwande," which means "growth" in the local language of isiNdebele, is the voluntary organization I founded and use to educate young women from peri-urban and rural areas of Bulawayo, Zimbabwe.

In the year 2023, I was selected for the Mandela Washington Fellowship for Young African Leaders, representing the one percent chosen from 75,000 applications across Africa.

This fellowship is a flagship of YALI (Young African Leaders Initiative), founded by President Barack Obama, and has grown to become one of the most prestigious fellowships for Africans by the United States of America.

**This** fellowship marked my first international travel and my first time on an airplane. Naturally, I was nervous, so I fully prepared for the journey to manage my anxiety.

I utilized the daily program agenda from the University of Notre Dame, where I was going to study, to assist me with packing. The agenda highlighted daily activities and suggested attire suitable for each activity. I also ensured there were no airline ticket changes by registering with the airline I was using to keep track of my flight.

Since I was going to live in America for seven weeks, I took courses that taught cultural norms in America to help me navigate potential culture shock.

There was a strong emphasis on the importance of punctuality, as Americans regard being late as offensive. We learned it's important to arrive on time for appointments, meetings, and social gatherings is a sign of respect. Also, Americans tend to have a larger personal space bubble compared to African cultures. So, it's important to be mindful of personal boundaries and not stand too close.

Recognizing and respecting these cultural differences is crucial when transitioning from African to American culture. I am glad I attended the advanced cultural training as it helped ensure smooth interactions and prevent potentially awkward or embarrassing situations.

**Nontuthuzelo Sisale**
**Mandela Washington Alumna 2023**
**Bulawayo Province, Zimbabwe**

# NAVIGATING INTERNATIONAL BUSINESS ETIQUETTE

*"Good business etiquette is the glue that holds people and businesses together.*
*It helps you stand out in a competitive world."*

### Eunice Leong-Tan, Author

Etiquette, often described as the set of customary rules and behaviors governing social interactions, plays a pivotal role in the world of business. Business etiquette generally includes polite speech and mannerisms, professional body language, consistent punctuality, following professional dress codes, and a well-groomed appearance. Business etiquette exists to preserve personal dignity and respect for others. [8]

Etiquette defines the way we communicate, negotiate, and build relationships with others. Yet, what constitutes good etiquette can vary significantly from one country to another. In the United States, for instance, business etiquette is deeply rooted in professionalism, punctuality, and a direct communication style.

However, as women entrepreneurs venture into the global arena, they soon discover that these norms can differ widely when doing business in other countries or with people who are from other countries traveling to the United States. Understanding these cultural nuances and adapting to diverse etiquettes is not merely a sign of respect; it's a strategic advantage in forging successful international business relationships.

---

[8] The Indeed Team. What Is Business Etiquette? (With Types And How To Improve) | Indeed.com India Published: September 2023.

## Why is international business etiquette important?

International business etiquette is an indispensable asset for women entrepreneurs looking to expand into the global market. Etiquette plays a role in fostering respectful interactions, building lasting relationships and ultimately achieving business success.

Here's why knowing international business customs is of such great importance:

**Setting the Tone:** Business etiquette lays the foundation for professional encounters. It creates an initial impression that can shape the entire course of a business relationship. A well-mannered approach sets a positive tone for interactions.

**Building Rapport:** Proper etiquette helps in building rapport and establishing a sense of trust and respect between parties. This interpersonal connection is essential for fostering successful business relationships.

**Effective Communication:** Etiquette facilitates effective communication. When everyone adheres to established norms, misunderstandings and communication barriers are minimized, leading to more productive exchanges of information and ideas.

**Enhancing Professionalism:** Demonstrating etiquette is a hallmark of professionalism. It showcases a commitment to conduct business in a dignified and respectful manner, reflecting positively on one's personal and corporate image.

**Cultural Sensitivity:** In an increasingly globalized business landscape, understanding and respecting cultural differences is paramount. Business etiquette takes these cultural nuances into account, ensuring that interactions are culturally sensitive and inclusive.

**Negotiation Success**: Negotiations are a common part of business dealings. Proper etiquette during negotiations can lead to more favorable outcomes, as it promotes a conducive atmosphere for reaching mutually beneficial agreements.

**Building Long-Term Relationships**: Etiquette fosters long-term relationships. It goes beyond transactional interactions and encourages a commitment to nurturing enduring partnerships, which can be invaluable for business growth.

### Scenario: The Business Meeting in Japan

Picture Sarah, a female entrepreneur from the United States, excitedly arriving in Japan for a crucial meeting. While she's well-prepared for business matters, she hasn't delved into Japanese cultural norms.

Sarah arrives on time for the meeting, as she usually does in the U.S., but the Japanese attendees consider her tardiness disrespectful. In Japan, punctuality is a sign of high regard.

When exchanging business cards, Sarah does so casually, unaware that it's a formal and respectful ritual in Japan. She misses the customary bow and the care taken when giving and receiving cards.

During the meeting, Sarah's direct and assertive communication style, typical in the U.S., clashes with Japanese preferences for subtlety and indirectness. Her straightforwardness is seen as abrupt and impolite.

By the meeting's end, Sarah's unintentional disregard for Japanese etiquette has left a negative impression. Her potential partners feel disrespected, highlighting the importance of cultural awareness for women entrepreneurs in the global arena. Understanding local customs can prevent such misunderstandings and foster stronger international business relationships.

As you can see, business etiquette is not merely a set of social niceties but a strategic tool that influences business success. It is the cornerstone of professional interactions, shaping perceptions, and laying the groundwork for fruitful collaborations. As the business world continues to transform entrepreneurs who recognize the importance of etiquette are better positioned for success in an increasingly interconnected global marketplace.

**Navigating Business Meetings and Negotiations**

In the realm of international relations, creating a favorable first impression is of paramount importance, as you typically only have one chance to get it right. Often, you have a mere three minutes to leave your mark. Here are some strategies to ensure you make a positive initial impact in any foreign or international market:

1. **Be Prepared:** Before your meeting, spend some time researching the country, culture, and traditions of your host or potential business partner. Since you'll be navigating unfamiliar territory, gaining insights into the local context is paramount. Neglecting this preparation could result in misunderstandings or leave an unfavorable impression. Let's say you are meeting with Japanese business colleagues, if you don't study up you would not know it is customary to bow, appropriate gift-giving protocols, and the importance of being on time are all important.

2. **Proper Use of Names and Titles:** Learn and utilize the correct names and titles when addressing individuals. In many cultures, names and titles carry significant weight and convey respect. In South Korea, addressing someone by their title, such as "Director Kim" or "Manager Lee," is considered polite and respectful.

3. **Appropriate Greetings:** Familiarize yourself with the customary greetings in the host country. Different cultures have distinct ways of greeting, and adhering to these conventions demonstrates cultural sensitivity. In France, a customary greeting involves kissing on both cheeks. Being aware of this practice can help you engage comfortably in social interactions.

4. **Basic Language Skills:** Make an effort to learn and use a few basic words or phrases in your business prospect's native tongue. Even a small linguistic gesture can foster goodwill and bridge communication gaps. For example, if you are conducting business in Brazil, learn how to say "Hello" and "Thank You", in Portuguese can go a long way.

5. **Respect for Personal Space:** Be aware of cultural norms surrounding physical closeness. In the United States having your own personal space (an arm's length apart) is important, it's essential to understand that in various countries, the acceptable distance can significantly differ. For example, in many cultures, people often stand closer during conversations to demonstrate warmth and attentiveness, which might contrast with the larger personal space preferred in the U.S. Understanding these differences is vital for successful international interactions.

6. **Understanding Local Business Protocol:** Study up on the local business protocol or meeting a potential international business partner for the first time. Learn what to expect during business meetings, appropriate negotiation tactics, and the decision-making processes. For example, in the United Arab Emirates, it's customary to offer coffee or tea when meeting with business associates. Familiarity with this tradition showcases your respect for local customs.

7. **Cultural Gift-Giving Etiquette:** Learn about the custom of gift-giving in the host culture. In many places, presenting appropriate gifts is a sign of respect and a gesture of goodwill. Take China for example, it's customary to give and receive gifts with both hands. Understanding this practice ensures you give and receive gifts respectfully.

8. **Punctuality:** Familiarize yourself with the host culture's attitude about time. Some cultures prioritize punctuality, while others have a more flexible approach to schedules. In Germany, punctuality is highly valued, so arriving on time or slightly early for meetings is a sign of professionalism.

By including these strategies in your approach, you can enhance your chances of making a positive first impression in international settings and building strong relationships with potential business partners.

**Business Entertaining and Social Etiquette**

When it comes to expanding your horizons as a women entrepreneur in the international business landscape, understanding the nuances of social etiquette is like unlocking the secret code to building meaningful connections and fostering lasting partnerships. Let's take a look into the essentials that can make your interactions truly shine:

**Understanding Social Customs and Traditions:** Each corner of the world has its own unique set of customs and traditions that influence social interactions. Take the time to explore and appreciate these cultural gems, as they can guide you in navigating various social scenarios with grace and respect.

**Appropriate Dress Codes and Attire:** Dressing the part is not just about fashion; it's a form of non-verbal communication. Discover the art of dressing appropriately for different occasions and cultures, ensuring that your attire speaks volumes about your respect for local norms.

**Dining Etiquette and Table Manners:** Breaking bread together can be a powerful way to build connections. Dive into the world of dining etiquette and table manners, mastering the art of shared meals and conversations that transcend borders.

As you embrace international business etiquette, remember that it's not just about following rules but about learning and enjoying the rich tapestry of global cultures. Each insight you gain will be a steppingstone towards becoming a confident and culturally attuned entrepreneur who thrives in any corner of the world.

### Embrace Global Opportunities

You may not know this, our amazing world boasts 195 unique countries, each with its own treasure trove of business possibilities.

Learning is the key to preventing those awkward stumbles that can cause embarrassment for both you and those around you. It's crucial to show unwavering respect for potential clients, vendors, and partners. To navigate this path successfully, seek guidance from experienced individuals who've been down this road before. Don't hesitate to ask for their advice and tap into their wealth of knowledge, taking valuable lessons from their past mistakes.

With each new culture you embrace, your entrepreneurial spirit will soar, growing connections that transcend borders. Embrace global opportunities with unwavering confidence and witness the world unfolding its wonders before you.

The world is waiting to witness your remarkable journey, and I have every confidence that it will be nothing short of extraordinary. Safe travels!

# 06

## Overcoming
## Financial Barriers

# MAKING YOUR SMALL BUSINESS BANKABLE: NAVIGATING SMALL BUSINESS MICROLOANS

### *"Money grows on the tree of persistence."*
### *Japanese Proverb*

*"Money grows on the trees of persistence"* is a metaphor, or comparison between the importance of hard work and persistence in achieving success and wealth. Let us begin by taking a quick look at the current trends regarding lending to women entrepreneurs.

You might be wondering what does bankable mean? When you say your business is "bankable," it means that your business has the qualities and financial stability that make it eligible and attractive to traditional lending institutions, like banks, for obtaining loans or financial support. This term holds particular significance in the context of women entrepreneurs, as they continue to face unique challenges and disparities in accessing the financial resources necessary to make their businesses "bankable" by conventional standards.

Let us jump right in by looking at women entrepreneur business lending trends. According to the "Megaphone of Main Street: Women's Entrepreneurship Report."[9] in the past year, when entrepreneurs sought financing, men had a slightly higher success rate, with 38% obtaining loans or equity financing compared to 31% of women. This report paints a vivid picture of the journey women entrepreneurs embark on in the realm of microlending, shedding light on both the challenges they face and the opportunities that

---

[9] SCORE Megaphone of Mainstreet: Women's Entrepreneurship Report.
https://www.score.org/megaphone-main-street-women%E2%80%99s-entrepreneurship-spring-2018

await them.

Both male and female entrepreneurs often sought financing for similar reasons, primarily linked to kickstarting or expanding their businesses. However, there is a slight difference worth mentioning men seemed to be more inclined to secure financing for the exciting venture of launching a new product, with 26% of them going this route, compared to 22% of women.

In the *"Report: Women Business Owners Face Gap in Lending, Federal Contracts."* [10] reveals a stark reality where women entrepreneurs, despite constituting 30 percent of all small companies, receive just $1 out of every $23 in small business lending. Furthermore, women often encounter higher rates of loan rejection or less favorable terms compared to their male counterparts.

Starting and growing a small business often requires access to capital. Let us explore the journey of making your small business "bankable" by qualifying for low-interest microloans in the United States to help make your entrepreneurial dreams a reality!

**What is a microloan?**

Microloans are your secret sauce for getting started in the business world. They are like little bundles of financial support, tailor-made for self-starters, fresh startups with modest capital needs, and small businesses with just a handful of team members. These loans are your boosters, and they come with super-low interest rates!

---

[10] Report: Women Business Owners Face Gap in Lending, Federal Contracts.
https://www.sbc.senate.gov/public/index.cfm/2014/7/report-women-business-owners-face-gap-in-lending-federal-contracts

Picture this: up to $50,000 to kickstart or grow your business venture. Who offers these gems? Well, mostly nonprofit organizations, and many of them have a heart for helping those who might face challenges in the traditional lending landscape. Think women, minorities, veterans, and folks with unique entrepreneurial ideas. And here is the icing on the cake – these nonprofits do not just hand you money. Nope, they are all about support, mentoring, training, and guidance to help you thrive.

Microloans are all about setting you up for success. These lenders are on a mission to empower small businesses. Microloans are worth looking into whether you are a woman with a groundbreaking idea, ready to launch your startup, or not quite ready for a traditional loan microloan might be worth looking into.

When it comes to securing a microloan, you have got a network of options at your fingertips, including community development financial institutions (CDFIs), nonprofit organizations, alternative lenders, and even traditional banks. These financial heroes are on a mission to propel your small business to new heights.

Now, let us talk about the U.S. Small Business Administration's Microloan Program,[11] a true game-changer. The SBA partners with nonprofit community-based lenders, affectionately called Microlender Intermediaries. These intermediaries are your bridge to those coveted microloans. You can borrow up to $50,000 through this program, with the average loan size around $13,000.

Wondering about interest rates? They typically range from 2.5% to 18% unless you are considered high risk. Each lender has a different set of guidelines along with the term of the terms to pay the loan

---

[11] U.S. Small Business Administration MicroLoan Program.
https://www.govloans.gov/loans/microloan-program/

back. No matter where you are, you will be working with your local lending organization, which makes things super accessible.

What is really exciting– it is not just about the loan. The primary goal of microloans lending institutions is to support the growth and development of your small businesses. You might be wondering how is that? In many cases they provide resources, mentorship, training, education, and the support you need that comes with setting you up for success from day one. So, whether you are just starting or taking your business to the next level, microloans can be your partners in this exciting journey of entrepreneurship!

**Microloans offer flexibility and can be used for various business purposes, such as**:

- **Working Capital**: Cover day-to-day operational expenses.
- **Equipment Purchase**: Invest in essential machinery or technology.
- **Inventory Expansion**: Increase product offerings and meet growing demand.
- **Marketing and Advertising**: Promote your business and attract new customers.
- **Hiring and Training**: Employ additional staff and provide training.

### Eligibility and Qualification Criteria

When embarking on the journey to qualify for a microloan, it is crucial to recognize that each lender has its own distinctive lending and credit criteria. While it is true that many prospective business owners may encounter requests for collateral and personal guarantees from intermediaries, it's also uplifting to know that there are specialized loan programs out there that can offer more flexible terms.

In this ever-changing world of business lending, it is important to connect with individuals who stay informed about the latest developments in microlending. I urge you to establish relationships with financial consultants and local lenders and approach alternative lending options with enthusiasm and a strong sense of purpose. These proactive measures can pave the way for meeting the requirements to secure a microloan and propel you closer to realizing your entrepreneurial aspirations.

Every lender wants you to demonstrate:

- Your business performance history. Have you been making money?
- Your payback plan. Do you have the money to pay back the loan?
- Projected business growth. Does your business have potential to grow over the next 3 years or the length of the loan?

In general, depending on the lender your loan application will be evaluated on some or all the following:

1. Your business credit score is known as "creditworthiness" – sometimes your personal credit score but not always.
2. Available collateral meaning something of value that you offer to a lender as a guarantee that you will repay a loan. Not all lenders require this.
3. Proof of revenue demonstrates your business is making money, cash flow, profit & loss plus forecasting projected rate of growth and earnings
4. Your business plan
5. Your team of advisors
6. How you plan to use the money

## The 4 R's of Microlending Preparation

Before applying for a microloan, it is essential to prepare your business to enhance your chances of approval and be ready to fully explain your business plan, your business moving forward, and your financial statements. Be professional, be ready for your appointment.

**Review Your Credit**: Check both your personal and business credit scores and address any discrepancies or negative marks.

**Refine Your Business Plan**: Ensure your business plan is comprehensive, outlining your objectives, strategies, and financial projections.

**Refine financial Statements**: Prepare accurate financial statements, including income statements, balance sheets, and cash flow projections.

**Reinforce Professional Network**: Build relationships with mentors, local business associations, and CDFIs to gain insights and guidance.

## Sorting Out Microlenders

**The Small Business Administration Microlending program** offers smaller-size loans of up to $50,000 provided through SBA funding intermediaries (banks). Proceeds from an SBA microloan cannot be used to pay existing debts or to purchase real estate. You could make a reference that there is a full list of authorized intermediary lenders on the SBA website. You can filter them by state.[12]

**Kiva** is a nonprofit microlender that works both globally and

---

[12] List of microlenders | U.S. Small Business Administration (sba.gov)

domestically, providing interest-free microloans of up to $10,000.

**Grameen America** is a microfinance institution that makes microloans to low-income women entrepreneurs.

**Opportunity Fund** mission is to provide business owners with small business loans, with a focus on business loans for women and minorities, who might not qualify for traditional financing.

**Community Develop Funding Institutions** (CDFIs) provide safe, responsible options when banks will not or cannot lend. We fill small business financing gaps, offering financing and technical expertise to help small businesses launch, grow, and succeed.

### Empowering Your Small Business Financially

For women entrepreneurs navigating the world of microloans is a valuable opportunity to secure the capital needed to fulfill those big dreams to upscale your business growth and secure success. By understanding the qualification criteria, preparing your business, and wisely using microloan funds, you can make your small business "bankable" and unlock its full potential. Remember that your entrepreneurial journey is unique, and with commitment, determination, and the right financial support, you can achieve your business dreams.

### Case Studies: Success Stories of Microloan Recipients

To inspire your journey, we will explore real-life success stories of small business owners who leveraged microloans to achieve their goals and elevate their enterprises.

*"Throughout my extensive experience working with Small Business Owners, one Borrower stands out vividly in my memory. His story is a*

*testament to the tremendous impact of the SBA, and it's a tale that I will forever cherish. This borrower was a disabled Veteran who had dedicated his entire life to saving for the purchase of the building in which he ran his business. I had the privilege of assisting him in securing an SBA loan that enabled him to turn his dream into reality by acquiring that property. This experience ranks among the most rewarding in my professional journey. It is precisely these moments that reinforce my deep admiration for individuals like Cindy Cohen, who provide unwavering support to Entrepreneurs and Small Business Owners."*

Stephanie Thomas, AVP, SBA, Relationship Officer – TORCH
First Savings Bank – Small Business Lending

*"I spoke with a client of mine. Sharon is an African American steel hauler in an industry prominently dominated by men and she is very proud of this fact. Sharon has been in the steel hauling industry for 4 ½ years. Sharon came to me recently for the first time for financing of a semi she stated "Applying was easy because I had my credit in line, and I have the savings in place as well to back me up. I was confident with my time in the industry and my finances. Stacey was excellent, resourceful, and knowledgeable to work with and knew the type of loan I needed for my business."*

Stacey Wing
Senior Retail Business Banker
1st Source Bank

# 6 Steps to Creating a Strong Business Profile

ONCE THESE STEPS ARE COMPLETED YOU ARE
READY TO APPLY FOR TIER 1 ACCOUNTS

**STEP 1**
Business Name: You must use your registered business name when applying for credit. Make sure ALL the information matches what's on your EIN & State Registration paperwork.

**STEP 2**
Business License: Make sure you check to see if your business will require a license.

**STEP 3**
Federal EIN: Use your EIN when applying for credit. Make sure the EIN information matches your state registration. If you need to apply for your EIN you can click the link below.
https://www.irs.gov/businesses/small-businesses-self-employed/apply-for-an-employer-identification

**STEP 4**
Physical Address: Use a business address either Brick and Mortar or Virtual. Do not use your home address as you will take the chance of your personal credit profile merging with your business profile. You DO NOT want this to happen, keep them separated. If you need a virtual address, see the link below. www.ipostal.com

**STEP 5**
Business Phone: Your business phone number must be a real business number. Not a personal cell phone or home phone. If you need a business phone line, choose from the below. www.ringcentral.com www.grasshopper.com

**STEP 6**
List Yourself: List yourself on 411 directories under your business name. Creditors will search 411 to see if you are listed. www.listyourself.net -Website: You need a professional website that reflects your brand. – Professional email address: You need to purchase a professional email address. Not yahoo, gmail, aol ect.
Example: info@lets-ride.biz is an example of a professional email address

Developing your credibility is crucial to receiving business credit approval. By having a solid business profile your company is set up to be fundable according to creditor requirements. The following are basic steps you can take to ensure trustworthiness must be satisfied for you to be granted business lines of credit

Chart created by
Tina Shalane MMS, Business Consultant
Fort Wayne, IN
for She Means Business

# Tier 1 & 2 Credit Application Guide:
## Elevate Your Financial Status

✓ APPLY FOR 3-5 ACCOUNTS.
✓ ALL ACCOUNTS MUST BE PAID ON TIME.
✓ DO NOT GO TO TIER 2 UNTIL EVERY ACCOUNT YOU APPLIED FOR IS REPORTING TO DUN & BRADSTREET.
✓ PAYDEX SCORE* WILL POPULATE WHEN STEPS HAVE CORRECTLY BEEN FOLLOWED.

### Tier 1 Credit Accounts

Crown Office Supplies: www.crownofficesupplies.com
Ecredable: www.ecredable.com
Grainer: www.grainger.com
Maverick Office Supplies: www.maverickofficesupplies.com
Shirtsy: www.shirtsy.com
Staples: www.staples.com
Quill: www.quill.com
The CEO Creative: www.theceocreative.com

*What is a Paydex Score?

A Paydex score is a business credit score, similar to your own personal credit score. It is issued by Dun and Bradstreet and represents how likely it is that your business will pay vendors and suppliers on time.

While your personal credit score ranges from 0 to 850, your Paydex score is between 0 and 100.

### Tier 2 Credit Accounts

Amazon Net 55 Business Account
Best Buy Business Credit
Dell Business Credit
Hertz Rent A Car
Floor and Decor

Floor and Decor
Lowes Account Receivables
Pitney Bowes Postage Account
Sam's Club Card
Verizon Business Account
Newegg

### Tier 3 Bank Cards

Amex
Bank of America
Capital
One Chase

Discover Credit Card
PNC
US Bank
Wells Fargo

Here is where you are able to get high-limit approvals if you have followed the proven wot work system.

Chart created by
Tina Shalane MMS, Business Consultant
Fort Wayne, IN
for She Means Business

# Debby's Journey

Breaking through financial barriers is like tackling a challenging puzzle. At first, it can feel like you're up against a giant mountain, and that can be pretty scary. But here's the thing, that fear can actually light a fire under you. It pushes you to think outside the box and get resourceful.

Don't dwell on what you don't have, focus on what you do have that you can build upon!

You will start finding clever ways to make the most of what you've got. It's about leveraging your talents, maintaining a good circle of influence, and exploring innovative ways to increase your earnings. This whole process turns that big scary mountain into a challenge that you're eager to conquer.

It's proof that even when money is tight, your hustle and creativity can lead to some seriously impressive wins.

Debby Canarini
Debby Canarini Business Coach
Knox, IN

## FROM INTIMIDATION TO INSPIRATION: THE ONE PAGE BUSINESS BLUEPRINT

*"You have the ability to write the blueprint for your own goals and decide how you want to pursue them.*
*If you allow others to do it for us, you will not achieve our full potential to be the best you can be."*

*Ellen J. Barrier, author and founder of Barrier's Books & Associates*

The idea of tackling a "business plan" might make you feel like you are teetering on the edge of a cliff, contemplating a leap into the unknown. Those thoughts of avoidance are completely natural. But here is the thing: if the prospect of diving headfirst into a full-blown business plan seems daunting, there's a more manageable starting point—the One-Page Business Plan.

In this wild world of growing a business, things can seem complicated. You have already done tons of research about your business industry, customers, and detailed money predictions. You have also most likely taken some entrepreneur small business classes on how to run a business. It all seems endless and can really make your head spin. Putting your business together is one thing, presenting it to someone else and staying on track is completely another.

But guess what? We've got a secret weapon for you: the One-Page Business Plan. It's like a superhero in the world of business planning. Why? Because it's super simple and can help you go from feeling scared to feeling excited about your business journey. So, let's board on this journey together and unveil the power of the One-Page Business Plan your blueprint to making your dream business happen.

The idea of tackling a "business plan" might make you feel like you are teetering on the edge of a cliff, contemplating a leap into the unknown. Those thoughts of avoidance are completely natural. But here's the thing: if the prospect of diving headfirst into a full-blown business plan seems daunting, there's a more manageable starting point—the One-Page Business Plan.

It's all about taking those baby steps while keeping a keen eye on the results. And here's the kicker: planning isn't just about crafting a grandiose document; it's about actively steering and managing your business towards success.

But why should you care about planning, you ask? Well, it's all about focus, priorities, and getting things done. Planning, when done right, helps you steer your business in the right direction. It sets expectations, tracks results, and helps you manage the gap between what you expected and what actually happened.

**Full Business Plan**

Before you get started, let's review the difference between a comprehensive complete  full business plan and the One-Page Business Plan model. First the name.

In the world of business planning, a comprehensive business plan often wears many hats and goes by various titles, such as the Full Business Plan, Long-Form Business Plan, Traditional Business Plan, Formal Business Plan, and many others depending what the plan is being used for.

But for our discussion today, let's refer to it as the "Full Business Plan."

Now, what truly sets this Full Business Plan apart is its depth and breadth, can span anywhere from 30 to 50 pages. It's a meticulous, in-depth exploration of your business's past, present, and future.

Full Business Plan solidifies:

- Every aspect of your business, from identifying the problem you are solving, and evaluating all elements of building a case for how your business will solve this problem in a unique way including market analysis to operational logistics justifying your business model as sustainable.

- Building a case for the sustainability of your business into the future through financial analysis, projections into the future to identify and describe growth potential.

- Clarifies long-term goals and strategies for your business's growth and sustainability.

A thorough and detailed full business plan proves invaluable in the following situations:

1. Seeking to obtain funding from venture capitalists, angel investors, banks, other financial institutions, and grants.

2. Securing strategic partnerships, describing multifaceted business models encompassing various products or services, a diverse customer base, or intricate operational processes.

3. Strategizing for expansion into new markets, complete with an evaluation of competitors and market dynamics.

4. Regulatory authorities mandate a comprehensive business plan for compliance and adherence to industry standards.

**One-Page Business Plan**

Now about the shorter version of the business plan. This plan is recognized by a variety of names, such as Simplified Business Plan, Short-Form Business Plan, Compact Business Plan, and others. You will refer to it as "One-Page Business Plan" for this chapter.

This plan is focused, streamlined, easy to read and efficient. The length of this short form business plan is one (1) page back and front of an 8.5 x 11 sheet of paper.

One-Page Business Plans are:

- A laser focus into your business. In your One-Page Business Plan contains these basic key elements like your business idea, the problem you are solving, target market, marketing plan, team, revenue model, and expenses.
- Easier, faster to create and are perfect for startups, small businesses, launching new products or services, or accelerate growth.
- Helpful to easily identify deficiencies in your business roll out and as you move forward in your business.

## A One-page Business Plan can be useful in the following scenarios:

1. Provide a brief introduction to your business launch, a unique concept, a program, service, or a product.

2. Ensure transparency and concentration within your team.

3. Present to potential partners or exploring collaborative opportunities, as well as seeking guidance from mentors and advisors.

4. Introduction to initial conversations with financial institutions and lenders.

5. Address marketing and public relations strategies.

Remember, a One-Page Business Plan doesn't replace  the Full Business Plan in situations where comprehensive details and extensive documentation are required. Instead, it serves as a practical tool for managing your business efficiently and effectively in various stages and scenarios.

## The big question, which should you choose?

Well, it depends on your business and where you are in your entrepreneurial journey. One of the benefits of any business plan is it helps to keep you focused on the most direct route to business expansion. If you don't have either, a One-Page Business Plan is a great place to start and can serve as an outline of your Full Business Plan. If you already have a Full Business Plan a One-Page Business Plan is more user-friendly, who wants to read a 30-page document?

That being said if you are:

- starting, testing the waters, or you have a small venture, One-Page Business Plan (short form) is the way to go. It's quick, practical, and helps you avoid overwhelm.

- seeking substantial funding, planning to scale big, or you are in a complex industry, a complete business plan is recommended. The complete business plan (long form) demonstrates your commitment and professionalism.

**One-Page Business Plan – Let's go!**

A good One-Page Business Plan acts like a road map with a series of steps that bring your strategy to life. The goal of this short version of the business plan is to  break things down into manageable milestones. Let us be honest, we're more likely to get things done when you have clear steps to follow. These steps are what you call strategies—the small decisions you make every day, like which marketing channels to use, identifying your target market, who to partner with, the progress you are making along your journey and so much more.

Your short form business plan starts here!

Note most One Page Business Plans include the following areas, this is the outline used by our mentoring class participants and accepted by local lending institutions.

**Company Description:** Let us kick things off by introducing your business. Tell us the name, when it was started and how long you have been in business, where it is located, and share a little about why you started this venture. Give us a brief history of your journey so far!

**Service Provided:** Now, let us dive into what you offer. Tell us about your awesome products and services. How do you make them? How long do they last? And most importantly, what needs do they fulfill in the community? You want to know all the juicy details!

**Mission and Vision:** Every business needs a mission and a vision. Your mission is all about the purpose of your business. What gets you out of bed every morning? And what is your grand vision for the future? You want to hear about the impact you are aiming to make!

**Problem Statement:** Identify the problem you are solving. What challenges are you tackling head-on? Give us a clear picture of the pain points your customers face and how your business provides a solution.

**Solution:** Time to shine the spotlight on your solution! Who are the lucky ones you are helping, and what exactly do you provide? Show us how you are making a difference and making lives easier or better. What makes your solution unique?

**Purpose:** List the top 3 key purposes of your business or non-profit organization. Think about the goals you are striving for. What do you hope to achieve? Let us jot down those purposes, one by one!

**Competition:** Who is your competition? What company is providing the same or similar services, and products, include where they are offering the same. Locally, nationally, or globally if it applies.

**Target Market:** Who are your ideal customers? Describe your customer segments and let us know if you are focusing on a specific geographical area, gender, ethnic group, or age of the person you message is for.

**Marketing and Sales Plan:** Okay, spill the beans on your marketing and sales strategies. How do you plan to spread the word about your products and services? What are the specific methods you will use to win over new customers. And what makes your offering stand out from the competition?

**Business Milestones:** Milestones are like checkpoints along your business journey. Take us through the important events in your company's history, from its launch to your exciting future plans. Give us dates and results achieved, include recognition, certifications, events, community volunteerism and funding.

**Notable Extras (optional):** Feel free to add some extras if they are relevant to your business. You might want to share your incredible team members and their key roles. If you have any glowing testimonials or community partnerships, that is important too. Nonprofits can include what you are looking for such as volunteers, donations, sponsorships. The headings would be "Team Members Key Roles" and "Community Partnerships" following "Business Milestones section.

**Finishing Touches:**
Sometimes it is the small things that make all the difference such double checking for typos, spelling, and grammar mistakes. Include a high-resolution logo up top, and the footer of the page should include your company name, website, email, and phone number. If you can squeeze into this one-page document, add a nice professional photo. Of course, social media links, blogs, online resume links. Do not forget to use high quality paper, a good printer and present in a nice folder with your business card to make the best 1st impression.

Keep in mind business plans are dynamic documents, which means they should evolve alongside your changing business purpose, vision, and trajectory. Your business plan deserves regular revisits and updates, ideally at least once a year, to foster and support the growth of your enterprise.

One Page Business Plane Worksheet (front and back)

The image is the format we use in the C2YHWI Women Entrepreneur Excellence mentoring, course and certification program.

| (Front of Page) | YOUR LOGO |
|---|---|

| **Your Name - Lean Business Plan** | |
|---|---|
| **Name of Your Business / Date started:** | |
| **Identity / About / History:** | |
| **Service provided:** | |
| **Vision and Mission** | **Problem Worth Solving**<br>What challenges does your company solve? |
| **Solution**<br>What challenges does your company solve? | **Purpose (nonprofit) or Competition (for profit)**<br>1.<br>2.<br>3. |
| **Target Market**<br>Who makes up your target audience? Who are your ideal segments, personas, or customers? | **Revenue streams / Sales Channels**<br>How will you get your product/service to customers? |
| **Team and roles**<br>Who is a critical part of your internal team (name/role)? | **Partners and resources**<br>Who else is supporting your venture/business? |

©2022 C2 Your Health Women's Initiative Inc.    www.C2YHWI.org   www.womenmoveforward.info

(Back of Page)

---

**What makes this business unique?**

---

**Milestones** What projects or tasks must be completed in order to reach your goals?

| Milestone 1 | Milestone 2 | Milestone 3 | Milestone 4 | Milestone 5 | Milestone 6 |
|---|---|---|---|---|---|
| Company Startup Date | Date | Date | Date | Date | Date |

---

| Your picture | About You (BIO) |
|---|---|
| | |

---

| Contact Information: | Company Logo |
|---|---|
| | |

---

**You may also add these categories:**
Testimonials
Community Activities
Awards

©2022 C2 Your Health Women's Initiative Inc.    www.C2YHWI.org   www.womenmoveforward.info

# 07

## Leveraging Technology and Marketing

# DIGITAL TOOLS AND PLATFORMS: FUELING BUSINESS GROWTH

*"I know firsthand the complexities of leading an enterprise through business and technology transformation. It takes intense focus, a strong drive, and a clearly communicated vision to inspire and take an organization from where they are, to where they need to be - or where they want to go."*

*Safra A. Catz, the co-CEO of Oracle Corporation*

No matter your personal sentiments or thoughts about digital media, one thing is certain: it's an unstoppable force that's firmly woven into the fabric of our lives. There's no reversing this digital revolution. If you are holding back on learning how to make the most of digital media until some hypothetical event magically turns it off, it's time to rethink your approach.

In the dynamic landscape of today's digital world, the use of digital tools and platforms has caused a profound and lasting transformation. It's like a story of evolution and adaptation, where businesses and individuals embrace the digital age to thrive and succeed.

These digital helpers are like unsung heroes. They have the power to change the way we do business, connect with others, and find success in the market. They are not just opportunities; they are like a special path for small businesses to not only survive but to thrive and make a lasting impact in their industries. Whether you are just starting your business journey with lots of ideas and dreams or you are a seasoned entrepreneur looking for new ways to succeed, embracing the digital world is a huge step toward achieving your goals. It's not just a change; it's a game-changing evolution that can take your business to new heights.

Safra A. Catz, the co-CEO of Oracle Corporation, once said, *"I know firsthand the complexities of leading an enterprise through business and technology transformation. It takes intense focus, a strong drive, and a clearly communicated vision to inspire and take an organization from where they are, to where they need to be - or where they want to go."* These words really speak to the challenges and opportunities that small businesses face in today's digital age. They show how important it is to have a vision, stay determined, and communicate effectively as you move toward a more digital and prosperous future.

So, what's the key to growing your business? It's not just about getting bigger; it's about using the right tools and strategies to reach your full potential. In a world where being connected online is super important, entrepreneurs who use digital tools have a big advantage.

These five digital platforms and tools cover essential aspects of digital marketing, from engaging with your audience on social media to optimizing your website for search engines and effectively communicating through email marketing. Tailor your choices to align with your specific business goals and target audience preferences for the most impactful digital marketing strategy.

## 1. Digital Marketing Mastery: Becoming a Pro at Online Promotion

Digital marketing is the foundation of a successful digital strategy. It covers all sorts of online platforms and tools. In today's digital age, it's really important for businesses to use digital marketing to connect with their audience.

Let's explore some key areas and suggest digital platforms and tools that can help boost your digital marketing efforts:

## Digital Platforms and Tools (Chart)

| | Platform Suggestions | Tools |
|---|---|---|
| Social Media | Utilize Facebook, Instagram, and LinkedIn for B2B businesses, or platforms like Instagram, Twitter, and Pinterest for consumer-focused products. | Employ social media management tools such as Hootsuite or Buffer to streamline content scheduling, analyze performance, and manage multiple social accounts efficiently. |
| Content Marketing | Establish a blog on your website and explore guest posting opportunities on industry-relevant websites. | Enhance your content marketing with tools like Grammarly for proofreading, Canva for creating visuals, and WordPress for blogging. |
| Search Engine Optimization (SEO) | Optimize your website for search engines, primarily focusing on Google. | Leverage SEO tools like SEMrush or Moz for keyword research, on-page optimization, and tracking your SEO progress. |
| Email Marketing | Create and manage email marketing campaigns using platforms like Mailchimp, Constant Contact, or ConvertKit. | Improve your email marketing with automation tools to personalize emails and segment your subscriber list for better engagement |

| | | |
|---|---|---|
| Pay-Per-Click (PPC) Advertising | Consider running paid advertising campaigns on Google Ads and Bing Ads | Tools: Optimize your PPC ad campaigns for better Return on Investment (ROI) with management tools like WordStream or AdEspresso. |

## 2. E-commerce Excellence: From Local to Global

E-commerce has democratized the world of retail, making it accessible to entrepreneurs of all sizes and industries. It's no longer reserved for tech giants; now, even small businesses can create seamless online stores that enable them to reach a global audience.

Here are strategies for launching your e-commerce platform, ensuring an exceptional customer experience, and optimizing your online sales channels. To help you navigate this dynamic landscape, here are some recommended resources, platforms, and reading materials:

**E-Commerce Platforms**:

- **Shopify:** A user-friendly platform that offers a range of customizable templates and features to create a professional online store. It provides tools for inventory management, marketing, and analytics.
- **WooCommerce:** A WordPress plugin that transforms your website into a fully functional e-commerce store. It's highly customizable and integrates seamlessly with various WordPress themes.
- **BigCommerce:** Known for its scalability, BigCommerce is suitable for businesses of all sizes. It offers features like

multi-channel selling, responsive design, and comprehensive analytics.

## Resources for Launching Your E-Commerce Store:

- Shopify Academy: Offers free courses and tutorials on starting and growing your online store, covering topics from product photography to digital marketing.
- **WooCommerce Documentation:** A comprehensive resource for setting up and managing your WooCommerce store, with guides on everything from installation to customization.
- **BigCommerce University:** Provides a range of resources, including webinars and guides, to help you make the most of the BigCommerce platform.

## Optimizing Your Online Sales Channels:

- **Google Analytics:** A powerful tool for tracking website traffic and customer behavior. It provides valuable insights to optimize your website and marketing campaigns.
- **Facebook Business Manager:** Manage your Facebook and Instagram ad campaigns, create custom audiences, and track performance to maximize your social media advertising efforts.
- **Email Marketing Platforms:** Consider platforms like Mailchimp, SendinBlue, or Klaviyo to build and manage email marketing campaigns that drive sales.

By exploring these resources, leveraging e-commerce platforms, and implementing customer-centric strategies, you'll be well-equipped to navigate the world of online retail and unlock the full potential of your e-commerce venture.

## 3. Data-Driven Decision-Making: Unlocking Insights

In today's digital age, data is nothing short of a secret weapon for entrepreneurs. The ability to collect, analyze, and interpret data has become a cornerstone of success in the business world. By embracing data-driven decision-making, you not only gain valuable insights but also empower yourself to make informed choices that can significantly impact your business.

It's important to consider the consequences of not collecting ongoing data. Here are five financial consequences of not collecting ongoing data:

- **Limited Financial Support:** Reduced access to loans, grants, and investor funding.
- **Missed Growth Potential:** Overlooking growth and market opportunities.
- **Inefficient Resource Allocation**: Poor allocation of budget and manpower.
- **Risks of Costly Decisions:** Increased potential for costly mistakes.
- **Competitive Disadvantage**: Falling behind competitors with data-driven strategies.

### Benefits of Utilizing Data-Driven Strategies

- **Unlocking Data's Power:** Data encompasses customer behavior, market trends, efficiency, and finances. Effectively used, it provides a holistic view to find strengths, weaknesses, and improvements.
- **Fine-Tuning Operations:** Data-driven strategies aid operations by tracking KPIs and industry metrics. Analyzing production times, inventory turnover, or

customer service response rates spotlights areas for increased efficiency.

- **Identifying Growth:** Data uncovers growth opportunities beyond process optimization. Analyzing data helps spot trends, customer preferences, and untapped markets. For instance, monitoring website analytics reveals high-demand products or services to capture more market share.
- **Gaining a Competitive Edge:** In a competitive landscape, data-driven strategies provide a significant edge. Continual data monitoring enables proactive decisions, anticipating market shifts and customer needs, fostering agility and innovation.
- **Measuring Everything for Growth:** Data-driven decision-making centers on measuring everything relevant. This includes customer satisfaction, website traffic, social media engagement, or sales conversion rates. Such data provides a feedback loop to gauge product or service quality and assess their impact on growth.
- **Economic Impact and Proof:** Data-driven decisions result in cost savings, increased revenue, and improved profitability. Demonstrating quantifiable results builds trust and credibility with investors, stakeholders, and potential partners, highlighting the value of data in entrepreneurship.

Data-driven decision-making is not a mere trend; it's a fundamental aspect of thriving in today's business world. By harnessing the power of data, you can navigate the complexities of entrepreneurship with confidence, make informed choices, and steer your business toward sustainable growth and success.

## 4. Utilizing a Digital Customer Relationship Management (CRM) Tool

Exceptional customer service forms the heart and soul of flourishing businesses. Embracing a CRM system empowers you to simplify communication, personalize interactions, nurture lasting customer relationships, keep track of appointments and effectively follow-up.

Admittedly, discussing CRM systems is not the most exciting topic, however, it will be exciting when you know you are controlling your business, and your business is not controlling you. So, as you move ahead, in this relaxing exploration diving right into how CRM tools can boost customer satisfaction and cultivate steadfast loyalty.

**Practical Business Illustration:** Picture yourself as the owner of a home and commercial cleaning service. Some of your customers schedule cleaning weekly, every other week, monthly or maybe only once a year for a big cleaning. Your customers represent the life force of your enterprise, necessitating a robust system to manage these invaluable relationships and varied cleaning schedules. Having a CRM system at your fingertips will help you to easily access customer contact details, monitoring communications, generating quotes, processing payments, and orchestrating follow-ups, organizing the cleaning schedule, all within a unified platform.

Three examples of CRM (Customer Relationship Management) systems:

- ✓ Salesforce: Salesforce is one of the most widely recognized CRM platforms in the world. It offers a wide range of features for sales, marketing, customer service, and analytics. Salesforce allows businesses to manage their customer data, automate tasks, and track leads and opportunities effectively.

✓ HubSpot CRM: HubSpot offers a user-friendly CRM platform that is popular among small and medium-sized businesses. It provides tools for contact management, email marketing, lead nurturing, and analytics. HubSpot CRM also integrates seamlessly with other HubSpot marketing and sales tools.

✓ Zoho CRM: Zoho CRM is a cloud-based CRM solution that caters to businesses of all sizes. It offers features for lead and contact management, sales automation, analytics, and multi-channel communication. Zoho CRM is known for its affordability and ease of use.

These CRM systems are just a few examples, and there are many other options available, each with its unique features and pricing plans to suit the needs of different businesses.

## 5. Automation Advantages: Working Smarter, Not Harder

As you have probably figured out by now automation is the key to efficiency and productivity. Whether it's automating email marketing campaigns, managing workflows, or simplifying administrative tasks, digital tools can help you save time and resources.

## Final Thoughts

As you venture into the unknow, keep in mind the digital era brings forth a universe of boundless opportunities for entrepreneurs! Technology is your trusty companion, not an enemy, and with the right attitude, a hunger for learning, and a willingness to adapt, you can fully unleash the potential of digital tools and platforms to supercharge your business growth.

Are you excited to set sail on this thrilling digital adventure? The time has come to turn your business dreams into sparkling realities in the magnificent realm of the digital age!

○ **NOTES:**

# ONLINE PRESENCE & SOCIAL MEDIA MASTERY

*"With Social Media so prevalent we're all extremely visible. Your prospective clients, your peers and your competition can drill as deep as they wish searching, reading, and gathering information online about you and posted by you without you ever knowing who's searching. Depending on what they find, your prospects may choose to do business with you or not."*

*Mari Smith, Premier Facebook Marketing Expert*

It often seems like everyone, and their beloved pets, funny kids, and scholarly advice have hopped aboard the social media train. There's a lot of competition out there. Before you dive in headfirst into the fast-paced world of tweets, likes, and shares, let's pause for a moment and ponder the question: Why are you on social media to begin with? By now you are deep in the growth stage of your business, so you've got down the basics, now is the time to catapult your brand into the digital stratosphere, weave unbreakable connections with your audience, supercharge your sales engine, or perhaps, unveil something entirely wild and unexpected? Understanding your purpose will serve as your roadmap to navigating the complex landscape of social media and harness its power to take your business to the next level.

## Making Your Social Media Presence Known

In the dynamic world of social media, start your journey with a map. Social media platforms are like bustling cities with unique populations.

Facebook, the grand metropolis, hosts over 2.8 billion monthly users. It's ideal for engaging with a broad audience, building a community, and fostering personal connections.

Instagram, the vibrant art district, boasts over a billion users. It's perfect for businesses with visual appeal, where stunning photos and stories shine.

LinkedIn, the polished business district with 700 million professionals, is great for B2B engagement. It's a platform for networking and industry discussions.

Twitter, the bustling newsroom with 330 million users, is perfect for wordsmiths offering quick insights and real-time updates.

Start by understanding your brand and your audience's preferences. Choose the platform that aligns with your business goals.

## Crafting an Irresistible Profile

Your profile is your digital identity, so make it count. Ensure a high-quality, consistent profile picture. Your description should convey your brand succinctly, incorporating industry-relevant keywords and a clear call to action.

Consistency is key; align your digital presence with your physical branding. Encourage cross-channel engagement by displaying social media handles on your website, email signature, and business cards.

Building a captivating social profile is just the beginning. Encourage customers and offline contacts to follow you on social media to expand your reach.

## Fueling Engagement with Fresh Content

**Stay Relevant:** Post about trending topics and current events that align with your brand and values.

**Be Consistent:** Craft a content calendar to maintain a steadfast presence with diverse, engaging content. Experiment with various formats like videos, images, articles, and infographics to cater to diverse tastes.

**Diversify:** Manage your content portfolio; consider posting content created by customers or users who have had experience with your business and want to share their thoughts, opinions or creative content related to building authenticity and community.

## Creating a Broadcast Schedule, Adopting a Distribution System

Now that you have the content, and a social media calendar, it's time to create a broadcast schedule to simply your journey. Your content schedule serves as the compass and a content management system (CMS) is your trusty guide. Check out Hootsuite or Buffer designed to you to schedule posts, manage content calendars, monitor performance metrics, and manage multiple platforms.

## Creating Trust and Authentic Connections

People prefer to do business with those they like and trust. Authenticity is the cornerstone of relationship-building on social media.

1. **Be the Master of Variety:** Share diverse content, from industry news to behind-the-scenes glimpses and user-generated content. Variety keeps your audience engaged.

2. **Foster Authentic Connections:** Focus on building genuine relationships. Provide value, solve problems, and engage in discussions authentically.

## Assessing Your Social Media Success

Understanding and evaluation are vital in social media marketing.

1. Understanding Your Audience: Start with profound persona research to tailor content to your target demographic.

2. Learning from Mistakes and Successes: Embrace mistakes as valuable lessons. Analyze both successes and failures to continuously refine your strategy.

3. Regular Assessment: Stay agile by assessing your content's performance. Identify what works and what doesn't to course-correct swiftly.

In the ever-changing world of social media, your adaptability and authenticity are your superpowers. Embrace your brand's uniqueness, connect wholeheartedly with your audience, and witness your business soar to new heights.

# 08

## Cultivating Resilience and Leadership

## SUPPORT, MENTORSHIP, AND LEADERSHIP RESILIENCE IN SCALING YOUR BUSINESS

*"Fearlessness is like a muscle. I know from my own life that the more I exercise it, the more natural it becomes to not let my fears run me."*

*Arianna Huffington, CEO Thrive Global*

Scaling your business is not a journey for the faint-hearted or those with small ambitions. It's a path marked by bumps, roadblocks, detours, and, at times, even setbacks. As you navigate this challenging terrain, you are bound to encounter moments that test your resolve. Yet, in this journey, you'll find the pillars of fearlessness, support, mentorship, and unwavering resilience.

Scaling isn't solely about expanding your business; it's also about personal growth and leadership development. It's about becoming the kind of leader who can confidently confront challenges and transform challenges into opportunities.

Picture it as a road trip where you not only build your business but also shape yourself as a leader who can stand tall in the face of adversity. Along this journey, we'll explore how to exercise your fearlessness muscle, overcome self-doubt, harness the power of support and mentorship, and understand that, just like a road trip, you are going to need a mentor as a guide to help navigate the path and leave behind the hurdles and setbacks, emerging stronger and wiser.

This isn't just about growth for growth's sake. It's about elevating your vision, expanding your reach, and making a more significant impact. Yet, it's a path fraught with obstacles, uncertainties, and moments when fear can creep in. That's why we're here—to guide you through this transformative journey. Do you have to have a business mentor? No, if you don't the journey will take much longer to get to your destination. If you don't mind, waiting for those big dreams, taking the scenic route might be better for you. Otherwise, keep reading.

We'll begin our journey by embracing Arianna Huffington's wisdom, allowing us to strengthen our fearlessness muscle, conquer self-doubt, and direct our energies toward building businesses that not only flourish but also serve as inspiration.

In the realm of entrepreneurship, success hinges on cultivating resilience and leadership. It extends beyond business growth and delves into gracefully navigating challenges while guiding our ventures to greater heights. Within this section, we'll delve into the synergy between scaling your business and the profound roles of support, mentorship, and resilience.

## The Importance of Scaling with Resilience

Resilience is the capacity to rebound and recover after facing setbacks. Scaling, on the other hand, is all about growth — expanding while preserving both your personal integrity and your business's core purpose. Think of cultivating resilience as the bedrock that equips you to endure the challenges that come with scaling. It's the ability to pivot when circumstances demand it, much like a tree that bends with the wind but stands tall and strong once the storm has passed.

## Identifying Growth Opportunities with a Resilient Lens

Adapting resilience into your skill set equips you to see opportunities even in the face of adversity. A resilient mindset empowers you to not only navigate challenges but also seek innovative solutions, think outside the box, and seize growth opportunities that may arise during the journey.

## Challenges of Scaling and Resilient Leadership

I am sure you have discovered by now scaling your business will come with its own set of challenges. But here's the deal: having a strong resilient leadership skill set is like having a secret weapon to overcome those challenges. It's kind of like this. Imagine you are running a tech startup that's growing fast, and suddenly, you hit a financial roadblock. To be a resilient leader means you can take a step back, look at the whole picture, figure out what to do considering your financial situation, and at the same time, keep your business's big goals in sight. A resilient leader will not see this as a sink or swim situation. It is you looking for your life jacket before you fall into the water, not after. Or maybe it is like being a smart captain who can steer a ship through tricky waters.

## The Role of Support Systems in Building Resilience

As you cultivate resilient leadership skills, you'll discover your inner savvy. You'll realize that you don't have to navigate the highs and lows of scaling alone, as you'll have your superhero support system and squad by your side.

Picture it like this: you are a superhero, I like the sound of that don't you, and your support system is your team of superhero sidekicks. Having mentors, business coaches, advisors, entrepreneur superstars and a skilled team is like having the best sidekicks ever. They bring their own superpowers to the table. Mentors and advisors can offer wisdom and guidance, like Yoda guiding Luke Skywalker. Your skilled team is like the Avengers, each member with their unique strengths.

So, when we talk about building a robust support system, we mean surrounding yourself with these amazing people who can help you tackle challenges and boost your resilience. It's like assembling your own superhero squad to take on whatever scaling throws your way. We'll explore how these skills and support networks can make you a super-resilient leader in the world of entrepreneurship.

## Mentorship as a Pillar of Resilient Scaling

It's super important to remember that not everyone makes a great mentor. Sometimes even well-meaning friends can unintentionally throw a wrench on your plans, and some folks might give you advice that isn't exactly on point. So, here's the deal: when you are looking for a mentor, it's like picking the right tool for a job. You want someone who's got the skills and experience to guide you on your journey.

Think of it like this: would you trust a chef to fix your car? Probably not, right? It's the same with mentorship. You want someone who's been there, done that, and knows the ropes. That's where certifications, endorsements, and training come into play. They' are like your GPS to finding the right mentor.

Mentors are like your personal guides on this epic scaling adventure. They've been through it all and can give you the inside scoop on what to expect. They share their own stories, the good and the not-so-good, to help you navigate the highs and lows of growing your business. So, remember, picking the right mentor is a big deal, and it plays a huge role in building your resilience and leadership skills.

**Resilience is a Mindset for Scaling Success:** A resilient mindset is an entrepreneurial superpower. We'll discuss how self-confidence, adaptability, and the ability to bounce back from setbacks are essential elements of a resilient scaling mindset.

**Measuring Resilient Success:** Scaling is a journey, and measuring success should include assessing your resilience. We'll explore how setting and achieving goals, tracking KPIs, and maintaining a resilient outlook contribute to your success.

As we wrap up this conversation let's circle back to Ariana Huffington's wise words about fearlessness being like a muscle. That muscle is your resilience, and your leadership is the compass guiding your business through the stormy seas of uncertainty. Remember, at the crossroads of scaling, embracing support, mentorship, and resilience, you hold the keys to unleashing your potential as a resilient leader in the entrepreneurial world.

This is a journey marked by growth, adaptability, persistence, commitment, and unwavering determination—and it all starts with you. So, fear not, embrace the challenges, and lead your business to success!

## Essential Skills for Scaling Entrepreneurs and Resilient Leadership

*Entrepreneurs scaling for resilient leadership need a diverse skill set*

**ADAPTABILITY**
Pivot quickly with changing circumstances

**PROBLEM-SOLVING**
Identify and solve issues efficiently

**FINANCIAL WISDOM**
Manage finances effectively, maximize profits

**RESILIENCE**
Bounce back from setbacks

**SKILL SET**

**STRATEGIC THINKING**
Set clear goals and plan for growth

**RESOURCES**
Manage and optimize resources

**COMMUNICATION**
Build strong relationships

**INNOVATION**
Embrace new ideas and tech

Chapter: 8 Support, Mentorship, and Resilience in Scaling Your Business
"She Means Business"
© 2023 copyright Cindy Cohen

174

# Traci's Journey

★ ★ ★ ★ ★

My role model was my mom. She owned a beauty shop and also my aunt who rented rooms out to people in the community. I owned Tee's Wear in 1994, back then no one was really talking about business mentors /coaches, well not to me, outside of the two very strong ladies that raised me.

When I closed in 1996 to take care of my mom I didn't give up my car and the garage was my business spots, to this day I continue to meet customers to keep the schedule going Cindy and I had conversations: What is the percentage of women-owned businesses? What do the numbers say for minority businesses in the community?

Well, Cindy was intrigued to find these numbers out and to also find these business owners in the community. Partnering with C2 Your Health Women's Initiative Inc. in 2018 was a true game changer in personal and business relationships then in 2019 Covid-19 happened. Just opening up a brick-and-mortar boutique was very interesting. I was shifting with several businesses BMWS & HOUSING LLC, Unique Boutique International LLC, Unique Juice Plus, and a nonprofit organization H.O.T. Hear Our Tears domestic violence awareness. Cindy Cohen is my mentor, Cindy said to me in early 2018 "Get that business plan, get QuickBooks now, get a bookkeeper, update that business plan and wear your buttons ask me about my business,"

Cindy noticed I was an introvert who needed to be bold and embrace what I was offering and helping people with my for-profits and nonprofits.

In the Women Move Forward Initiative, a dynamic collaboration has taken shape, uniting C2YHWI and The Pokagon Fund. Together, they've crafted the Women Entrepreneur Women Move Forward Mentoring Online Community, while also launching the H.O.T Domestic Violence Community Ambassador program. This initiative not only educates our community on how they can contribute but also integrates vital domestic violence support into the mentoring program.

The partnership has been nothing short of remarkable, leading to the discovery of a multitude of talented entrepreneurs within our community. It's with great excitement that Cindy and I came together to form the Women Move Forward Initiative. This initiative is designed to provide much-needed support for women in domestic violence environments, and alongside our thriving entrepreneur mentoring membership community, it paves the way for greater entrepreneurial business resilience on my journey.

As Cindy always says: "I can help you with that or I know someone you should have a meeting with to help your business." Making an impact for all women business entrepreneurs has grown my community. With the team of mentors and coaches and success connections, resources inspiring entrepreneurs my business continues to flourish and grow.

Through engaging in mentor group discussions, attending meetings, and participating in training sessions, I've gained a wealth of knowledge. The experience has been invaluable in my pursuit of scaling my businesses, including Unique Boutique International, LLC, H.O.T Hear Our Tears for domestic violence awareness, and BMWS and Housing, LLC. The guidance and support from our amazing mentors and coaches have been a tremendous source of inspiration and motivation, driving me forward on my journey towards continued success in business.

Traci Winston Williams
Unique Boutique Internationa LLC
H.O.T. Hear Our Tears - Founder
South Bend, IN

## NURTURING MENTAL HEALTH AND EMOTIONAL INTELLIGENCE

*"Success is not about climbing up the ladder,*
*it's about how satisfying the journey is to you and how*
*well you're able to balance your work, your life, your*
*family, your interests, your passions, your priorities.*
*It's about taking care of your well-being and*
*your mental health."*

*Arianna Huffington, CEO Thrive Global*

Arianna Huffington's quote underscores that success in business is not solely defined by professional achievements but also by how well individuals manage their well-being, including their mental health. It emphasizes the need for balance and self-care as integral components of a successful entrepreneurial journey.

You are like the heart and soul of your business, its driving force, and its future. Imagine your well-being as a powerful tool that can help you save time, stay productive, and make more money. It's like this: if you are not feeling good, it's tough to be happy.

More than ever, I am hearing women business owners & entrepreneurs complain of increased feelings of anxiety, worry and depression. Maybe this is you too? You might be surprised to know you are not alone in this boat.

Many women business owners and entrepreneurs are feeling more anxious and depressed lately. You are not alone. A study by the Canadian Mental Health Association and the Business Development Bank of Canada found that 62% of business owners feel depressed weekly. They are stressed about money (67%) and personal responsibilities (39%). Over half feel inadequate (51%) and down (50%).[13]

The solution may be simpler than you think. Take care of your mental well-being and emotional intelligence, just like tending a garden. Explore your thoughts, nurture your emotions, and adopt healthy habits. Manage stress like a gardener trimming a garden.

Remember why you started your business, whether for family time or freedom. It's time to reset and recharge for personal growth and success. We'll uncover connections between these elements and strengthen your leadership skills on this exciting self-improvement journey.

As you go about your busy life and work, it's important to take a moment to remember why you started your business in the first place. Do you want more time with your family? Or perhaps you dreamed of being your own boss, having the freedom to take vacations and do things your way? Well, guess what? It might be time to hit the reset button, relax a bit, and recharge your batteries.

By doing this, you are setting yourself on a path to build a strong and balanced foundation for your personal growth and success in your journey as an entrepreneur. You've totally got this!

**The Role of Mindset**

Think of mindset as your very own superpower – it's like having a magical pair of cool glasses that change the way you see the world.

Picture this: You wake up in the morning and put on these incredible glasses called a "positive mindset." Suddenly, everything

---

[13] Michael Guta. 62% of Business Owners, Feel Depressed Once a Week. Small Business Trends. Smallbiztrends.com Published: September 20, 2021

around you look a little brighter. Challenges don't seem so daunting anymore; they start to resemble exciting puzzles waiting to be solved. With your positive mindset glasses on, you become a bit of a superhero. You can spot opportunities where others might see roadblocks.

Imagine, you are driving down the entrepreneurial highway, and there's a detour ahead. With your positive mindset glasses on, you don't see it as a roadblock, but rather as a scenic route full of new adventures and discoveries.

So, remember, your mindset is like the lens through which you view the world. Having a positive mindset is like having cool glasses that help you spot opportunities even in challenging situations. I like to think of it as putting a positive spin on every situation in life. Whatever happens keep those glasses on, no matter what, look through them as you explore this exciting world of entrepreneurship with an open heart and a positive outlook!

**Nurturing Emotional Intelligence**

Now that you have your special magical cool glasses, you need a trusty compass pocket as you set out exploring your exciting adventure of entrepreneurship. Whether you are in a dense forest or a dessert island when you have this magical compass that not only points in the direction you want to go, but it also helps you to navigate the tricky trails of personalities and decision-making.

Just like that compass, emotional intelligence is your secret weapon. It's your guide through the maze of emotions, helping you understand not only your own feelings but also those of the people around you. Your compass along with your special pair of magical glasses that allow you to see beyond words, right into the hearts and minds of others.

When you nurture your emotional intelligence, you become a master at decoding the unspoken language of body language and emotions. You can empathize with your team, read your customers' needs like an open book, and make decisions that resonate with the people who matter most to your business.

With emotional intelligence as your trusty sidekick, you'll be unstoppable in the world of business!

### Building Healthy Lifestyle Habits

Harvard Health Publishing Harvard Medical School published *Nutritional Psychiatry: Your Brain on Food*[14] using this description how food impacts your mental health.

Here's what they said.

*"Like an expensive car, your brain functions best when it gets only premium fuel. Eating high-quality foods that contain lots of vitamins, minerals, and antioxidants nourishes the brain and protects it from oxidative stress — the "waste" (free radicals) produced when the body uses oxygen, which can damage cells.*

*Unfortunately, just like an expensive car, your brain can be damaged if you ingest anything other than premium fuel. If substances from "low-premium" fuel (such as what you get from processed or refined foods) get to the brain, it has little ability to get rid of them. **Diets high in refined sugars, for example, are harmful to the brain**. In addition to worsening your body's regulation of insulin, they also **promote inflammation and oxidative stress**. Multiple studies have found a correlation between a diet high in refined sugars and impaired brain*

---

14 Eva Selbub,MD. Nutritional psychiatry: Your brain on food - Harvard Health, Harvard Health Review. Published: September 18, 2022

*function — and even a **worsening of symptoms of mood** disorders, such as depression."*

Surprised? This leaves you with the question to ask yourself "Am I making my anxiety and depression worse? If so, what can I do about it?" The solution to positively impacting those feelings of anxiety and depression could be as simple as looking at your everyday food choices.

*"Start paying attention to how eating different foods makes you feel — not just in the moment, but the next day. **Try eating a "clean" diet (loaded with fruits, vegetables, nuts, seeds)** for two to three weeks — that means cutting out all processed foods and sugar. See how you feel. Then slowly introduce foods back into your diet, one by one, and see how you feel.*

*When some people "go clean," they cannot believe how much better they feel both physically and emotionally, and how much worse they then feel when they reintroduce the foods that are known to enhance inflammation."* [15]

So, are you still unsure which choices are best for your plate? Look to the USDA/My Plate website www.choosemyplate.gov for healthy lifestyle suggestions. When making lifestyle choices focus on the "4 Pillars of Health" 1. Drink water 2. Stay active 3. Get sleep / Reduce stress 4. Eat real food. The USDA recommends 6 cups of fruits and vegetables per day, if this is too hard The Juice Plus Company has a high quality, well research, whole food supplement available www.wholefood4you.com. Check out the One Simple Change program.

---

[15] Cindy Cohen RN, BS BA. Women Entrepreneurs: 62% feel depressed at least once a week (c2yhwi.blogspot.com), Support Her Journey: C2 Your Health Women Entrepreneur Initiative Experience. Published: April 2021

Can't do it alone? Consult someone who knows about whole food nutrition, clean eating, a healthcare professional such as a dietitian, nutrition expert or certified health coach.

## Resilience and Mental Health

As you conclude this journey of discovering how to strengthen your mental well-being, don't forget to welcome the realms of resilience and mental health into your life. Together, they form an unwavering partnership, ready to support you through any challenges that come your way!

Close your eyes. Visualize your life as a thriving garden, with you nurturing a magnificent tree of resilience. When those life storms roll in – and they will – your mental health acts like those sturdy, anchoring roots. These roots keep you grounded during tough times and provide the strength to withstand even the fiercest winds.

The enchanting part of it all? Just as a tree grows taller and more magnificent after each storm, your resilience grows stronger with every challenge you conquer. It's like crafting a suit of armor from your experiences and self-care, always ready to shield you from whatever life sends your way.

Think about this, as you keep cultivating that garden of personal growth and success, know resilience and mental health are your trusty companions on this incredible entrepreneurial journey. You've got this!

- **Blueprint for**
- **Changing**
- **Your**
- **Mental**
- **Health**

Physical gestures
of warmth from yourself
can tap into your inner
caregiving system
activate caregiving
system.

## Step 4

## Step 3

Reframe the
observations
made by your inner critic
to more positive,
forgiving words.

## Step 2

## Step 1

Soften the self-critical inner voice, notice self-judgement, show yourself compassion, release self-judgement.

Begin to notice when you are being self-critical, validate or dismiss with a reality check.

Source: self-compassion.org

# Balancing Act:
# Top Tips for Managing Work, Home,
# and Mental Health Stress

## Adopt Healthy Behaviors

 Evaluate the Source of the Stress and Anxiety

Accept the Uncomfortable Feelings You're Having

Communicate Your Boundaries Clearly

Say "no" more often than not

Take Time Off For Yourself to Reload Your Batteries

## Develop These Healthy Habits

 Choose healthy food, plant-based, mostly fruits and veggies. unhealthy foods put your mind and body in a stressed-out state. Recommendation 6 cups F & V are natural stress reducers.

 Get 6 - 8 hours of sleep per night, have a bedtime routine, best sleep is before 10 pm. Sleep improves memory, maintains body weight, boosts immune system.

 Drink water approx. 1/2 your body weight in oz. For example: If you wt. 100 lbs. the amt. you would drink is a minimum of 50 oz/day. Water improves mood and brain function by helping it to produce the chemical serotonin the 'feel-good' natural medicine for your brain.

 Stay active to improve your mood. Endorphins, are your brain's feel-good natural medicine administered during activity. The more often you exercise the more you will feel less stressed.

Chart created for She Means Business
© 2023 Cindy Cohen

# 09

## Giving Back and Creating Impact

## EMPOWERING CHANGE THROUGH PURPOSE-DRIVEN GROWTH

*"The purpose of life is not to be happy. It is to be useful, to be honorable, to be compassionate, to have it make some difference that you have lived and lived well."*

*Eleanor Roosevelt, former First Lady of the U.S. and human rights activist*

As Eleanor Roosevelt beautifully reminds us, *"The purpose of life is not to be happy. It is to be useful, to be honorable, to be compassionate, to have it make some difference that you have lived and lived well."* These words serve as a guiding light as you embark on your journey, exploring the world of purpose-driven initiatives. Here, you will uncover the remarkable ways in which you can leverage your entrepreneurial spirit to make a profound impact on the world through your business endeavors. This voyage is nothing short of exhilarating, for it aligns your ambitions with a higher purpose, a path eagerly embraced by a growing community of entrepreneurs committed to creating positive change.

**Why Purpose Matters**

Have you ever considered that an average person spends a significant portion of their life, approximately 1,842 hours each year, working? That's a staggering total of 92,100 hours over the course of a 50-year career. However, amidst the hustle and bustle of our professional lives, it's all too common to lose sight of the fundamental reasons behind our actions. Or maybe we never really identified the reasons, or our purpose?

It's crucial to recognize that research unequivocally supports the idea that both you and your business or organizations experience greater fulfillment and improved performance when you are driven by a genuine sense of purpose. To illustrate this point, let's explore five compelling studies that shed light on the profound significance of purpose in our lives and work. According to deou.com in an article published *"5 Studies on the Benefits of of a Purpose Driven Workplace"*[16] according to the study having a sense of purpose in our life is critical to well-being. In fact, in a longitudinal study (meaning over time), researchers found that people who demonstrate a sense of purpose in their lives have a 15% lower risk of death compared with those who said they were more or less aimless. It didn't seem to matter how old you are when you found your direction or purpose. It could be in their 20s, 50s, 70s. Surprised? Me too!

But why does purpose matter? Why should you consider doing business on purpose

**A Good Look and Feel**

When your business operates with a clear sense of purpose, it radiates authenticity and integrity. It's not just about profits; it's about making a positive impact. This authenticity resonates with your customers and employees alike. People are drawn to people and businesses that stand for something more than their bottom line. It creates a good look and feel – one that sets you apart in a world where genuine purpose is valued more than ever.

**Motivated Employees**

Your employees are not just there to collect a paycheck; they want to be part of something meaningful. When your business embraces

---

[16] 5 Studies on the Benefits of a Purpose Driven Workplace. IDEOU.
https://www.ideou.comBe/blogs/inspiration/5-studies-on-the-benefits-of-the-purpose-driven-workplace

purpose-driven initiatives, it gives your team a sense of pride and motivation. They see that their work is contributing to greater good, which can lead to increased job satisfaction and loyalty.

In that same article *"5 Studies on the Benefits of of a Purpose Driven Workplace"* also reported was the *2015 U.S. Purpose Index study* found that purpose-oriented employees have 64% higher levels of fulfillment in their work.[17]

If you belong to the millennial generation, here's an intriguing tidbit: a remarkable 84 percent of this group prioritizes making a meaningful impact in the work they choose over seeking professional accolades. But, for all of you who fall outside the millennial category, you've probably observed a noticeable shift in work values since the onset of the pandemic.

It's no longer just about clocking in and out; it's about deriving profound satisfaction from your job, leaving a positive mark on your community, embracing challenges for personal growth, and feeling genuinely valued. The traditional desire for mere management has given way to a hunger for leadership, the pursuit of significance, and, of course, financial success. Frankly, who wouldn't want to pursue such a rewarding combination? So no surprise, research from Deloitte shows that "mission-driven" companies have 30 percent higher levels of innovation and 40 percent higher levels of retention. [18]

**A Community Connection**Beyond your business's four walls, the community at large benefits from your purpose-driven endeavors.

---

[17] 2016 Workforce Purpose Index.
https://cdn.imperative.com/media/public/Global_Purpose_Index_2016.pdf
[18] Becoming Irresistible: A new model for employee retention. Deloitte.
https://www2.deloitte.com/us/en/insights/deloitte-review/issue-16/employee-engagement-strategies.html

It's not just about what you sell; it's about the positive change you create. This builds a deeper connection with your community, establishing your business as a valued contributor to its well-being.

## Finding Your North Star

At the heart of any purpose-driven initiative is a clear and compelling purpose. Take a moment to reflect on your business – what is it that truly inspires you? What cause or mission speaks to your heart? For instance, Soulful Kitchen and Hope for the Hungry are prime examples of how a catering business can merge with a hunger relief nonprofit to create a powerful force for good. Soulful Kitchen not only serves delicious meals but also helps combat food insecurity in their community.

## Partnerships that Propel

Partnerships are the rocket fuel for your purpose-driven initiatives, and the best partnerships benefit both parties. When considering partnerships, think about choosing a private-public partnership where both entities share the same values and target market. Sometimes, partnering with a small non-profit can be an excellent strategy because both of you are highly motivated – you gain new customers and them to increase donations and volunteers.

Partnerships are just good business. In the book, *Firms of Endearment,* the authors built an 18-firm index of purpose-driven companies and tracked their financial performance over 10 years. They found showed an average annual return on equity of 13.1% — that's 9% higher than the S&P.[19]

---

[19] Rajendra S. Sisodia, David B. Wolfe, Jagdish N. Sheth. *Firms of Endearment. How World-Class Companies Profit from Passion and Purpose.* February 2007.

Here is a short list of why this approach is particularly beneficial:

### ✓ Shared Values, Common Goals

In a successful partnership, shared values and common goals serve as the foundation. When both your business and your partner organization are aligned in terms of values and mission, your collaboration becomes a powerhouse of purpose. It's not just a transaction; it's a transformation.

### ✓ Tapping into Each Other's Strengths

Partnerships allow you to tap into each other's strengths. Your business might bring expertise, resources, and marketing reach, while your partner organization may bring community trust, passion, and local insights. Together, you create a synergy that can achieve far more than either of you could on your own.

### ✓ Expanding Your Reach

By partnering with organizations that share your target market, you can dramatically expand your reach. Your partner's audience becomes your potential customers, and vice versa. This approach isn't just about increasing your bottom line; it's about making a greater impact together.

### ✓ Mutual Motivation

Small non-profits are often highly motivated to grow their reach and impact. By collaborating with them, you not only help them achieve their mission but also benefit from their determination and passion. They can become strong advocates for your business within their networks and you for theirs withing your network. When your partnership leads to increased donations and volunteers for your non-profit partner, you are contributing to the greater good. These organizations are often the lifeline of many communities, addressing critical needs and offering support where it's needed most.

### ✓ A Ripple Effect

By forming these partnerships, you are not just benefiting your businesses – you are creating a ripple effect that touches countless lives. The positive change you initiate can inspire others to follow suit, and together, you are shaping a community that cares and collaborates.

So, consider private-public partnerships and collaborations with small non-profits when incorporating purpose-driven initiatives into your business strategy. The benefits are mutual, the impact is profound, and together, you can create lasting change.

### The Community Connection

Your purpose-driven initiatives can ripple out to touch every corner of your community. Take Women's Entrepreneur Matter and their partnership with the City of South Bend's Alive Grant and Milestone Academy LLC, supported by Angels of Integrity Youth and Family Services LLC. This dynamic alliance is committed to uplifting families and youth in low-income neighborhoods. These collaborations demonstrate the transformative power of purpose-driven entrepreneurship.

These partnerships say a lot about you as a business owner and your company. They show that you are not just focused on profits; you are deeply committed to creating positive change. It highlights your company's values and its dedication to the well-being of the community you serve.

## What Matters

On your purpose-driven journey, it's important to measure your impact. Keep track of the lives you touch, the changes you bring about, and the progress you make toward your mission. Impact metrics can be a source of motivation and a testament to the difference you are making.

A purpose-driven organization can measure success through metrics such as social impact, employee engagement and satisfaction, customer loyalty and satisfaction, and financial performance. Success is not only measured by profit but also by the positive impact your business or organization is making on your community locally and globally.

## Resources for Your Journey

Here is a list of podcasts to listen to, books to read, and brands to follow to assist you with your purpose-driven path. These resources are here to support you in creating a business that makes a difference.

Podcasts to listen to:

- ✓ Yes! You Can
- ✓ Brave + Boss
- ✓ Why's Words
- ✓ The Business of Meaning

Books to read:

- ✓ Green Giants
- ✓ The Purpose Economy
- ✓ Social Movements for Good

✓ Unstuck & Unstoppable: Shake Off the Past, Find Your Purpose, Get on with Your Life

Inspiring purpose driven brands to follow:
- Patagonia
- Ben & Jerry's
- LUSH
- IKEA
- Adidas

Just as discovering purposeful meaning for your business can create value for your business, living a purpose driven life will help you discover meaning in your personal life. As you uncover the many benefits that ripple through not just your professional realm, you will also uncover what makes you, and what you need to create personal meaning. It's nothing short of magical!

Research, as showcased in Forbes.com in the article *"4 Steps to Measuring the Power of Purpose in Your Organization "*[20] unveils this transformative power of purpose for business, organization, and individuals.

For individuals, leading a purpose driven company and living a purpose driven life is like discovering a secret elixir:

- ✓ It adds precious years to our journey.
- ✓ It becomes our shield against the specters of heart attacks and strokes.
- ✓ It wards off the looming shadows of Alzheimer's.
- ✓ It paves the path to serenity during the day and peaceful slumber at night.

---

[20] 4 Steps to Measuring the Power of Purpose in Your Organization. Jim Ludema and Amber Johnson. Forbes.com. Apr 2, 2021 https://www.forbes.com/sites/amberjohnson-jimludema/2021/04/02/four-steps-to-measuring-the-power-of-purpose-in-your-organization/?sh=416fc2e61c71

- ✓ It doubles the odds of staying drug- or alcohol-free after treatment.
- ✓ It boosts our good cholesterol, fortifying our well-being.
- ✓ It weaves the threads of better personal relationships into the tapestry of our lives.

And above all, it gifts us the immeasurable treasures of meaning, engagement, life satisfaction, and boundless happiness.

The article goes on to say, "in the words of the wise Dr. Bob Quinn, the author of *"The Economics of Higher Purpose"* and the visionary founder of the University of Michigan's Center for Positive Organizations, *"You and I are designed to be purpose-seeking mechanisms."* [21]

It's a journey of self-discovery, a quest for fulfillment, and a pathway to embracing life's most profound joys. As mentors, we cherish not just professional growth but the profound transformation it brings to our very essence.

**Overcoming Challenges**

Remember, the path of purpose may come with challenges. You might encounter skepticism or resistance but stay true to your mission. Many successful purpose-driven entrepreneurs have faced obstacles on their way to making a significant impact. Learn from their stories and keep moving forward.

**Be Inspired**

To end on a high note, here are a few inspiring quotes from

---

[21] 4 Steps to Measuring the Power of Purpose in Your Organization. Jim Ludema and Amber Johnson. Forbes.com. Apr 2, 2021 https://www.forbes.com/sites/amberjohnson-jimludema/2021/04/02/four-steps-to-measuring-the-power-of-purpose-in-your-organization/?sh=416fc2e61c71

entrepreneurs who have embraced purpose:

*"The thing that is really hard and really amazing is giving up on being perfect and beginning the work of becoming yourself." — Anna Quindlen, Co-Founder of "The Quilt," a social platform for cancer patients.*

*"Purpose is the reason you journey. Passion is the fire that lights your way." — Unknown*

*"Do not bring people in your life who weigh you down. And trust your instincts ... good relationships feel good. They feel right. They don't hurt." — Oprah Winfrey, Media Mogul and Philanthropist.*

*"Life-fulfilling work is never about the money — when you feel true passion for something, you instinctively find ways to nurture it." — Eileen Fisher, Founder of Eileen Fisher Inc., a clothing company focused on sustainability.*

*"The work that I do — finding and developing meaningful work that is in service of others — has been the most important thing in my life. My work is my purpose." — Jacqueline Novogratz, Founder of Acumen, a nonprofit global venture fund.*

*"The success of every woman should be the inspiration to another. We should raise each other up. Make sure you are very courageous: be strong, be extremely kind, and above all be humble." — Serena Williams, Tennis Champion, and Entrepreneur.*

These quotes reflect the wisdom, passion, and purpose-driven mindset of accomplished women entrepreneurs. Their words are not only inspirational but also serve as a testament to the importance of embracing purpose in one's entrepreneurial journey.

## The Purpose Driven Wheel IDEO[22]

From a mentor's perspective, we have an inspiring tool called the Purpose Wheel, This ingenious framework was crafted by IDEO to help organizations discover their sense of purpose. The journey towards purpose begins by brainstorming the many ways an organization can make a positive impact on the world.

The Purpose Wheel guides discussions about future aspirations, laying the foundation for an organization's leadership to unite around a common purpose asking at each stage of the wheel *"Why do we exist beyond making a profit?"* At the heart of this wheel, we find five distinct avenues through which a company or organization can influence the world. The outer rim of the wheel is designed to stretch your imagination and compel you to explore how your company can create a meaningful impact. It's here that you'll continue crafting your purpose statement: *"We exist to (as determined by the inner wheel) through (as envisioned by the outer wheel) to make a positive difference in society."*

This is a powerful tool to clarify and crystallize your organization's mission, and it's the first step on the path to making a real impact in the world. Peter Fisk has this list of purpose driven companies on the website: [23]

- ✓ We exist to Enable Potential ... Creating impact by inspiring greater possibilities. (Tesla, Nike)
- ✓ We exist to Reduce Friction ... Creating impact by simplifying and eliminating barriers. (Google, Spotify)
- ✓ We exist to Foster Prosperity ... Creating impact by supporting the success of others. (Pampers, Warby Parker)
- ✓ We exist to Encourage Exploration ... Creating impact by championing discovery. (Airbnb, Adobe)

---

[22] The Purpose Wheel by IDEO - Peter Fisk
[23] The Purpose Wheel by IDEO - Peter Fisk

## The Purpose Driven Wheel by IDEO (Chart) [24]
### Peter Frisk, Business catalyst. Keynote speaker. Expert advisor.

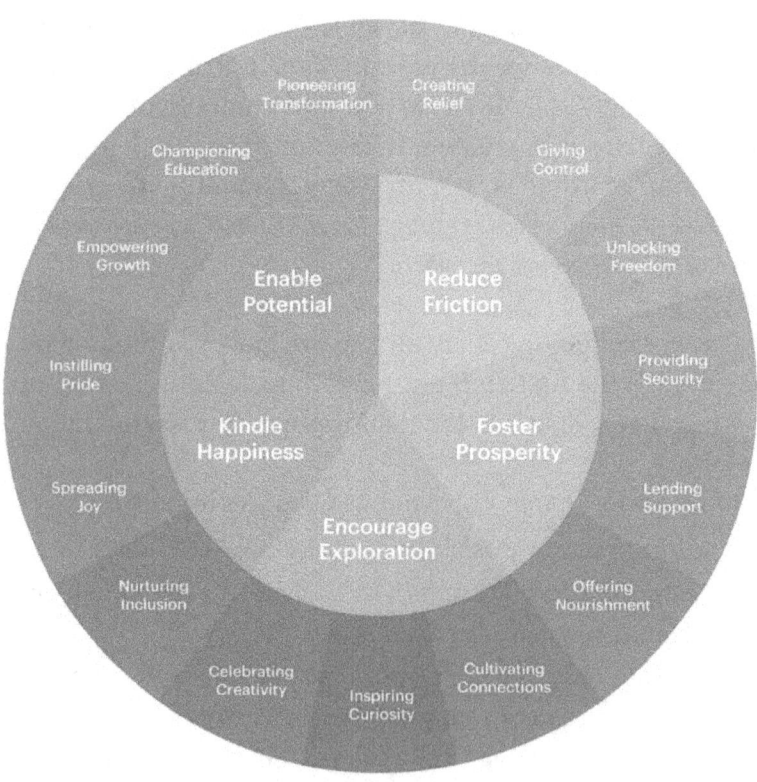

[24] The Purpose Wheel by IDEO - Peter Fisk

# Ylonda's Journey

★ ★ ★ ★ ★

Being part of the women entrepreneur community has been a game-changer for my business. The unwavering support, mentorship, and diversity within this community have fueled my entrepreneurial journey with invaluable knowledge and inspiration.

It's a sisterhood that breaks down barriers and fosters innovation. Moreover, it's instilled a sense of purpose, leading me to support other women-owned businesses and mentor aspiring entrepreneurs, creating a ripple effect of positivity.

In essence, this community has not only strengthened my business but enriched my life. With its unwavering support and inspiration, I'm soaring higher than ever before.

Together, we're changing the face of entrepreneurship, and the future is brighter than ever!

Ylonda Scott, CEO
**Personal & Business Development Coach**
**SheBoss Oasis Retreats & Conferences**
Niles, MI

## ENRICHING YOUR COMMUNITY
## THROUGH SOCIAL IMPACT

*"A woman with a voice is, by definition, a strong woman.
But the search to find that voice can be
remarkably difficult."*

*Melinda Gates, Co-founder Bill and
Melinda Gates Foundation*

This quote emphasizes the importance of finding your voice and using it to empower your community to create positive social change. This quote underscores the idea that when women speak up and take action, you can make a significant impact on your community and the world at large.

In the realm of women entrepreneurship, the impact of individual and community support extends far beyond the individual success stories. It creates a ripple effect that radiates through communities, fostering profound social change. As Melinda Gates so wisely put it, *"A woman with a voice is, by definition, a strong woman."* When your find your voice and come together with other women you can use your voices to empower change. When many voices come together and the likelihood of being heard is multiplied exponentially and incredible things can happen.

So, get ready to explore the powerful journey of other women entrepreneurs and the positive influence you bring to the world around you!

1. **Economic Empowerment:** Exciting times are ahead for those who are truly passionate about their mission and are ready to aim

for the stars! According to a recent Forbes[25] article, the world of women entrepreneurship is on the rise, and the future is looking brighter than ever. In the U.S. alone, we witnessed a remarkable surge with women launching 1,821 net new businesses every single day last year. And here's something truly incredible: 64% of these newly minted women-owned businesses were initiated by women of color, making 2023 a year of diversity and empowerment.

But that's not all; the growth stats are even more astounding! Latina women-owned businesses, for instance, saw an incredible surge of over 87%. If we go back two decades, we find that there are 114% more women entrepreneurs today than there were back then. Investors and venture capital firms are catching on, starting to recognize the potential of women-led startups.

That's not all governments, organizations, and communities are rallying behind women entrepreneurs, offering unprecedented support and resources to fuel their dreams. Look around in your community open your eyes to how communities are coming together to see the emergence of ecosystems that are tailor-made to nurture women entrepreneurs, and there's a beautiful trend of grassroots mentoring programs and networking meetups created by women for women. These aren't just support systems; they are empowering platforms for personal growth and success. The stage is set for women entrepreneurs to shine and make their mark on the world!

2. **Inspiring Future Generations:** Women entrepreneurs shine as guiding lights, inspiring future generations. Your daughters and granddaughters are observing, absorbing, and gaining wisdom from your journey. When young girls witness the women in their

---

[25] Women Entrepreneurs Poised For Growth In 2024 (forbes.com). **Melissa Houston.**

community achieving entrepreneurial success, it sparks a profound belief in their own potential. This newfound inspiration broadens the horizons of our youth, revealing opportunities previously unseen and paving the way for a surge in aspiring women entrepreneurs.

Example: Rachel, a thriving school psychologist, draws inspiration from her mother's entrepreneurial journey, witnessing the multitude of rewards it brings. She envisions entrepreneurship as her path to a future where she can embrace flexibility, care for her family's needs, and build an income that aligns with the quality of life they desire.

3. **Community Revitalization:** In many urban areas, women entrepreneurs have played a crucial role in community revitalization. They establish businesses in underprivileged neighborhoods, creating opportunities for local residents and stimulating economic growth.

**Example:** Octavia's journey is an incredible example of resilience and entrepreneurship. Starting with making face masks in early 2020, she quickly moved to a storefront, which she eventually purchased and renovated. But her journey didn't stop there. Octavia's boldness led her to inquire if the building owners were open to selling, plunging her into a whole new realm. Suddenly, she found herself navigating contracts, banks, and loans, handling renovations and lease negotiations. It was during this time that she discovered something called "incremental development," a unique approach to revitalizing declining neighborhoods. Octavia's story is a testament to the power of ambition, adaptability, and the transformative impact of entrepreneurial spirit in reinvigorating communities.[26]

4. **Social Impact Initiatives:** Women entrepreneurs often initiate and support social impact projects within their communities. They fund scholarships, promote environmental sustainability, and address pressing social issues through their businesses.

Example: Cindy's incredible initiative is all about creating a social impact. She's the driving force behind a non-profit organization that is dedicated to uplifting women entrepreneurs from low-income neighborhoods and those affected by domestic violence. Her organization operates on a foundation of mentoring and resource connections, extending a helping hand to women who need it the most.

But that's not all; they are not just about providing assistance from the top down. They are all about grassroots action. Through networking, workshops, and empowerment, they are mobilizing women in the community to stand together and support one another. Together, they are making a powerful statement, raising awareness about the unique challenges women face and working to eliminate gender bias in their community. Cindy's vision is a true testament to the change one person can bring to the world.[27]

5. **Networking and Collaboration**: Supportive communities enable women entrepreneurs to form valuable networks and collaborations. These collaborations can lead to innovative solutions to local challenges and boost the collective success of businesses.

---

[26] Octavia Ray. South Bend's micro-scale developers are changing this Indiana city (jsonline.com). Mary Hall. Published: South Bend Tribune February 2022
[27] Cindy Cohen. C2 Your Health Women's Initiative Inc. www.C2YHWI.org

Example: is a true catalyst for positive change. She envisioned a powerful networking group aimed at empowering, inspiring, and supporting women and women entrepreneurs across four neighboring communities. By actively engaging and supporting the women entrepreneur network, she found her own path to entrepreneurship.

Now, Stacey is on a mission to launch her own business venture, complete with a co-working space and a business incubator. This collaborative environment has been the nurturing ground for numerous startups, contributing to remarkable economic development within their community. Stacey's journey is not just about her own success; it's about uplifting an entire ecosystem of women entrepreneurs and fostering the growth of their local community.[28]

6. **Representation in Leadership**: Women entrepreneurs often take on leadership roles in community organizations and chambers of commerce. Their representation ensures that the unique needs and perspectives of women-owned businesses are considered in local policies and initiatives.

Example: Shannon, owner of a women entrepreneur business serves as the founder, and president of the local faith-based women's entrepreneur group to gather for networking group to uplift, educate, share, connect and inspire each other to grow in every area of life. Her advocacy has led to increased community resources. [29]

As you can see, the ripple effect of community support for women entrepreneurs in our community, the U.S. and internationally is a

---

[28] Stacey Oberly Black. Michiana Women Rise. Facebook: Michiana Women Rise.
[29] Shannon Petty. Michiana Women Entrepreneur Alliance. Facebook Group.

force of positive change. It drives economic empowerment, inspires future generations, revitalizes communities, fuels social impact initiatives, encourages networking and collaboration, and ensures representation in leadership. As women entrepreneurs continue to thrive and uplift their communities, they leave an enduring legacy of empowerment and progress. Together, we rise to build a brighter and more inclusive future for all.

## The Magic of Community Building

Editor's note: Through years of observation and experience, it becomes evident that when women entrepreneurs unite with a collaborative entrepreneurship focus, something magical unfolds.

The synergy created in such gatherings can impact women in four keyways:

1. **Sisterhood:** The sense of belonging and coming together as sisters in entrepreneurship creates a powerful bond. This unity provides a strong support system that extends beyond business challenges.

2. **Empowerment:** Connecting with like-minded individuals who are on a similar path empowers women entrepreneurs. Drawing strength from one another, you find the resilience needed to overcome hurdles and pursue your dreams with vigor.

3. **Idea Sharing:** Collaboration within a community of women entrepreneurs fosters innovation and problem-solving. Sharing ideas and insights leads to creative solutions and business growth.

4. **Improved Sustainability:** Economic impact is a natural outcome of women entrepreneurs collaborating within a community. As your business and businesses around you thrive, you begin to see

how you contribute to the overall economic sustainability of your community.

**Final Thought: Embrace the Power of Community**

In conclusion, the journey of a woman entrepreneur is not one to be traversed alone. The power of community and social impact is undeniable. By participating in community-building activities such as women entrepreneur conferences, workshops, networking events, meetups, and organizations that support women in business, you can positively impact your business's bottom line, foster its growth, and achieve the success you aspire to.

This has been an empowering year in our community, as we came together to proclaim and celebrate the global movement of *Women Entrepreneurship Day*[30], November 19th. It's a day dedicated to recognizing the incredible contributions of women entrepreneurs in our community. They are the driving force behind job creation, economic growth, and so much more. Additionally, we're thrilled to share that two of our local women-owned businesses received well-deserved recognition from *Notre Dame University's McCloskey New Venture Competition*, marking them as not just good ideas but also fundable ones. These achievements are a testament to the incredible entrepreneurial spirit in our midst.

Furthermore, our ecosystem has been enriched with the addition of new programs and services. It's all part of a collaborative effort, and they are working harmoniously to empower women entrepreneurs and further boost our community's growth. The world is waiting to witness your remarkable journey, and there is every reason to

---

[30] Women Entrepreneurship Day proclaimed Nov. 19th by Mayor Dave, Common Council of Mishawaka, IN, Mayor John Mueller, Common Council, South Bend, IN, Mayor Rob Roberson, Mayor of Elkhart, and Eric Holcomb, Governor of Indiana 2022.

believe that it will be nothing short of extraordinary. Embrace global opportunities, thrive in your community, and make your mark on the world. Enjoy the journey.

# 10

## Empowered Entrepreneurship for Lasting Impact

## ERADICATING BIAS: PAVING THE WAY FOR WOMEN ENTREPRENEURS

*"I've seen over and over how much self-belief drives outcomes. And that's why I force myself to sit at the table, even when I am not sure I belong there – and yes, this still happens to me. And when I'm not sure anyone wants my opinion, I take a deep breath and speak up anyway."*

*Sheryl Sandberg, Chief Operating Officer (COO) Meta Platforms*

As you venture further into the world of woman entrepreneurship, it's essential to recognize the pervasive existence of bias – whether it takes the form of gender bias, community bias, or other variations. Bias might reveal itself through subtle yet impactful means, subtly shaping decisions, opportunities, and outcomes. Nevertheless, there's no need for concern; this chapter is dedicated to empowering you with strategies to conquer these challenges rather than dwelling on them.

Picture success as a mountaintop. The path to that summit may be steep, but it's not meant to be insurmountable. The weight of bias can make that ascent feel heavier, but it doesn't have to hold you back. By addressing and conquering bias, you are not just leveling the playing field; you are unleashing your full potential for success. As a result, the journey becomes not just about reaching the summit but about the remarkable growth you experience along the way.

Take a minute to think about taking Sheryl's words to heart, summon your self-belief, and get on board, we'll take this transformative journey together. It's time to force yourself to sit at the table", voice your opinions, and pave the way for your own success, regardless of the biases that may be on your path.

## What Unconscious Bias Looks Like

Imagine standing in front of a vast and magnificent forest. At first glance, it appears welcoming, with its towering trees and lush foliage. Yet, as you venture deeper, you start to notice the hidden undergrowth, the tangled roots, and the uncharted terrain that can trip you up when you least expect it. Unconscious bias is like that dense undergrowth, often concealed, but ever-present, in our entrepreneurial journeys.

Unconscious bias is the subconscious judgments and prejudices that we unknowingly hold deep inside us based on factors like gender, race, ethnicity, or even community ties. These biases subtly influence our decisions, interactions, and perceptions, often in ways we don't consciously recognize.

For women entrepreneurs, unconscious bias can manifest in the following ways:

**Gender Bias**: In the business world, gender bias can take various forms, such as disbelief about women's leadership skills, questioning their credibility as entrepreneurs, doubting their dedication to business ventures, or the outdated belief that women should prioritize homemaking over entrepreneurship. These biases often lead to women entrepreneurs being excluded from opportunities and receiving less financial support than their male peers.

For instance, a woman may be passed over for a leadership role due to the misconception that women are less capable leaders, while a male entrepreneur might receive more substantial funding for a similar business idea.

**Community Bias**: Community bias comes from preconceived

thinking that ties you to where you come from, the networks you belong to, or your cultural background. This shows up as a lack of trust or credibility, hindering access to resources and connections vital for business growth.

## Unconscious Bias Impact to Women Entrepreneur Growth

Imagine unconscious bias as an invisible hurtle on the edge of a dense forest that stands in your way as you strive for business growth. This invisible hurtle distorts perceptions and can make the path ahead seem uneven and unsafe. However, it's important to remember that even the densest forests can be navigated with the right tools, knowledge, and support. While unconscious bias may present a hurtle, it's one you have the ability to overcome as you forge ahead on your entrepreneurial journey toward success.

Here are the 5 most common hurtles:

1. **Access to Funding**: Women entrepreneurs often face challenges in securing funding for their businesses. Studies have shown that women receive a disproportionately smaller share of venture capital and angel investor funding compared to their male counterparts. This lack of financial support can hinder business expansion and development.
2. **Networking Opportunities**: In many industries, access to influential networks is crucial for business growth. Women may encounter barriers to networking opportunities, including exclusion from male-dominated circles or events. Limited networking can impede access to potential clients, partners, and mentors.
3. **Unequal Opportunities**: Women may face discrimination in various aspects of business, including access to opportunities, business building resources and partnerships that drive growth.

4. **Access to Markets**: Bias can affect how women's products or services are received in the market. Some consumers may have biases against women-led businesses, impacting market penetration and growth potential.

5. **Market Opportunities:** Bias can influence which markets or industries women feel comfortable entering. It may discourage them from pursuing opportunities in male-dominated sectors where significant growth potential exists.

Overcoming these barriers requires concerted efforts from both individuals and your community. Initiatives focused on promoting gender equality, diversity, and inclusion in entrepreneurship are essential for breaking down these obstacles and fostering an environment where all entrepreneurs, regardless of gender, can thrive and contribute to business growth.

### Empowering Change to Overcome Bias and Thrive in Entrepreneurship

As you gain new understandings remember that change begins with awareness. Start by recognizing instances of bias, no matter how slight or obvious, in your own entrepreneurial journey. Identify how bias appears in business transactions, decisions, or interactions and contemplate how to turn these situations to your advantage.

The next crucial step is to initiate a conversation about bias within your community forums and among fellow entrepreneurs. By discussing bias openly, we can collectively raise awareness and inspire change. Over time, your actions can lead to a shift in mindset and behavior within your community and the broader entrepreneurial landscape. While community efforts are significant, individuals also hold the power to drive change. You can contribute to creating a more inclusive entrepreneurial ecosystem.

**Now, let's explore how you can actively participate in this movement for change:**

- **Share Knowledge**: Share this book, its insights, and lessons learned with your peers, friends, and family. Keep yourself updated about bias and inclusivity. Knowledge empowers you to recognize and challenge bias when you encounter it.
- **Self-Reflection:** Take time to reflect on your own biases. Acknowledge them without judgment and work towards changing any biased behaviors or attitudes you may hold.
- **Practice Inclusivity:** In your business practices, prioritize inclusivity. Treat everyone with fairness and equality, regardless of their gender or background. Lead by example, and your actions will inspire others.
- **Engage in Conversations:** Don't shy away from discussions about bias and inclusivity. Share your knowledge and experiences with others and be open to learning from their perspectives.
- **Support Women Entrepreneurs:** Seek out and support women-owned businesses. Your support will make a big difference in their success just like it will for yours,
- **Support and Mentorship:** Extend your hand to support fellow entrepreneurs, particularly those who face bias. Mentorship, sponsorship, or simply offering encouragement can make a significant difference in someone's entrepreneurial journey.
- **Advocate for Change**: Use your voice and influence to advocate for change within your community and industry. Encourage others to join you in creating a more inclusive environment.

By taking these actions seriously you can become an active participant in the movement to increase awareness and break down barriers that hinder the success of women entrepreneurs. Success is attainable for everyone, regardless of gender or background.

## Surviving to Thriving - Breaking Barriers

Never forget, you deep inside you, you possess the strength and resilience to navigate the complex landscape of gender and community bias as a female entrepreneur. While challenges may arise, you have the strategies and support to thrive despite the many barriers ahead. Embrace the power of your unique perspective and experiences, for they are valuable assets on your entrepreneurial journey.

Always remember that success knows no gender or background. The path may have its twists and turns, but with determination, persistence, and a network of support, you can achieve your goals and shatter any barriers in your way. Seek out resources, mentors, and fellow entrepreneurs who understand your journey and can provide guidance and encouragement. Lock arms and travel the journey together.

You are part of a vibrant community of women and minority entrepreneurs who are rewriting the rules of business and creating lasting impact. Your vision, innovation, and determination are driving forces for positive change. Embrace your role as a trailblazer and let your entrepreneurial spirit soar. With every step you take, you pave the way for others to follow.

The future of entrepreneurship is diverse, inclusive, and brimming with potential. By staying true to your vision, continuing to learn and grow, and supporting one another, you can break down the barriers of bias and create an entrepreneurial ecosystem where every voice is heard, and every dream is realized.

Keep striving, keep thriving, and keep shaping the world through your entrepreneurial endeavors. You are unstoppable, and the world is waiting to witness your remarkable journey.

## Resources

In the pursuit of breaking through barriers and thriving as women entrepreneurs, knowledge and empowerment are our greatest allies. To equip you on your journey, here is a collection of invaluable resources. Whether through insightful podcasts, illuminating books, or informative blogs, these tools will serve as beacons of support to guide and fuel your entrepreneurial success.:

## Podcasts:

1. **Female Startup Club** is an interview-style podcast that features the actual experiences of female founders. You'll get first-hand feedback on how they built their businesses from the ground up, the hurdles they overcame, the challenges they continue to face, and the goals they've set for themselves and their business.
   https://www.femalestartupclub.com/

2. **Unfinished Biz Podcast** you'll gather insights on how to take the reins in startups, overcome various challenges with sound strategies, and treat your team so they will be encouraged to contribute significantly to the business. This podcast also highlights the value of setting time aside for your own health and well-being.
   https://www.unfinishedbiz.com/

3. **Boss Files Podcast** features interviews with global leaders, CEOs, entrepreneurs, and business honchos. The podcasts dive into their unique experiences and how their best practices and strategies paved the way for their businesses to get ahead of the game.
https://edition.cnn.com/audio/podcasts/boss-files

4. **The Guilty Feminist** comedian Deborah Frances-White and her guests explore feminism and its impact on women's lives, including entrepreneurship.
https://guiltyfeminist.com/

**Books:**

1. *"Lean In: Women, Work, and the Will to Lead"* discusses empowering advice for women in the workplace and insights into overcoming bias.
2. *"Five Second Rule"* leads you to become more confident, stop procrastinating and self-doubt, be fear, feel happier, get more done.
3. *"Atomic Habits"* is about improving yourself every single day. Practical strategies for forming healthy habits, breaking bad habits and creating new behaviors that lead you to the results you have been dreaming of.
4. *"The 12 Week Year: Get More Done in 12 Weeks than Others Do in 12 Months"* focus and clarity on what matters most and a sense of urgency to do it now. In the end more of the important stuff gets done and the impact on results is profound.
5. *"The 4% Fix"* shares with you the latest research on how to improve your time management and goal setting.
6. *"How to Win Friends & Influence People"* guides you through the six ways to make people like you and the twelve ways to win people to your way of thinking.

## Blogs and Websites:

LeanIn.org - Provides resources, articles, and research on gender bias and empowerment in the workplace and entrepreneurship.

Female Entrepreneur Association - A community and blog with articles, videos, and courses focused on helping women entrepreneurs succeed. femaleentrepreneurassociation.com/

Forbes Women - A dedicated section of Forbes featuring articles and insights on women in business and leadership. forbes.com/forbeswomen

Girlboss - An online community and blog offering career advice, entrepreneurship stories, and resources for women. girlboss.com/blogs/read

Support Her Journey: The C2 Your Health Women's Initiative Experience – We champion a remarkable journey—one that embodies entrepreneurship, mentorship, and holistic well-being. C2YHWI.blogspot.com

These resources can offer valuable guidance, inspiration, and strategies for women entrepreneurs looking to overcome gender and community bias and thrive in the business world.

## Comparing How Male and Female Entrepreneurs Are Described by Venture Capitalists

These gendered personas are illustrated with quotes from Swedish government VC's who were observed discussing a total of 125 applications for funding between 2009 and 2010.

| The average MALE entrepreneur is described with attributes such as: | The average FEMALE entrepreneur is described with attributes such as: |
|---|---|
| "Young and promising" | "Young, but inexperienced" |
| "Arrogant, but very impressive competence" | "Lacks network contacts and in need of help to develop her business concept" |
| "Aggressive, but really good entrepreneur" | "Enthusiastic, but weak" |
| "Experienced and knowledgable" | "Experienced, but worries" |
| "Very competent innovator and already has money to play with" | "Good-looking and careless with money" |
| "Cautious, sensible, level-headed" | "Too cautious and does not dare" |
| "Extremely capable and very driven" | "Lacks ability for venturing and growth" |
| "Educated engineer at a prestigious university, has run a business before" | "Visionary, but with no knowledge of the market" |

Note: Quotes were translated from Swedish to English.
Source: *"Gender Stereotypes and Venture Support Decisions: How Governmental Venture Capitalists Socially Construct Entrepreneurs' Potential"*. By Malin Malmstrom ET AL., Entrepreneurship Theroy and Practice, February 2017.

# Nyauhango's Journey

I stand as a testament to the remarkable journey of success against all odds. I have always been driven by unwavering faith, self-identity, and an unyielding sense of pride,which has made me defy bias and emerged triumphant. In a world where prejudices could have hindered my progress, my unwavering belief in God, my abilities and uniqueness propelled me forward. Through perseverance, I have shattered barriers and gained recognition for my exceptional culinary skills, captivating the hearts from diverse backgrounds. My Kate's Kitchen serves as a beacon of inspiration, reminding us that with faith, self-identity, and pride, one can overcome any obstacle and achieve remarkable triumphs.

Nyauhango Wakwa Kaunga
Kate's Kitchen
South Bend, IN
Malawi, Africa

# EARNING TRUST AND REGOGNITION: THE POWER OF CERTIFICATION AND AWARDS

**"The question isn't who's going to let me;
it's who's going to stop me."**

## Ayn Rand, Author

As we come to the end of our journey in "She Means Business," I want to share my personal experience regarding the power of credibility, authority, and turning the tides in your favor. There's nothing trivial about being nominated for an award, winning one, or earning a certification. Each accolade serves as a vital building block, elevating your credibility and, by extension, the credibility of your small business. They act as a seal of approval, affirming your expertise, the quality of your services, or products. When your business is recognized with certifications or awards, it sets you apart from the competition, instills trust among potential customers, and firmly establishes you as an industry leader.

I admit that I didn't fully grasp the power of awards and certifications in the early days of growing my entrepreneurial business. It took me a while to gain confidence and truly see the value in earning these accolades.

When I was laser-focused on hyper-scaling my wellness business, C2 Your Health LLC, I concentrated on building the credibility that would distinguish my business, infuse respect as a small business owner and women entrepreneur, and establish public confidence, credibility, and authority in the wellness industry. To achieve this, I embarked on a journey to build credibility in the worksite wellness sector of C2 Your Health LLC. I earned certifications in worksite wellness, received certification from the benchmark corporate wellness company, WELCOA, earned eight certifications, and secured a faculty position at WELCO University. My efforts were further acknowledged when I received the DISH Award for innovative ideas in wellness and was honored with the Top 50 Health Promotion Professional Award for wellness education innovation, beating out over 300 applicants.

In addition, I began a blog and a weekly Wellness Wednesday newsletter, Nutz4Nutrition Blog, which gained significant popularity. I was even invited by Lee Saltz to contribute a chapter about "Networking" in his book, "Expert Guide to Small Business Success." From struggling to write just one chapter, I gained the confidence to write my first book, "Self-Marketing Handbook for Women Online and Offline." This success led to more books, blogs, magazine articles, and ezine articles. This was a significant achievement for me as I had experienced a major writer's block. These books became my "big business card," as leaving a book with a potential client carries a different weight than just leaving a business card.

Now, when I am nominated for or receive a personal or business award, I know it's a game changer. It's not just about me; it's about the work we're doing in the community. These accolades provide me with the courage to break through the gender and community biases that exist on my side of the table and among my potential partners and customers on the other side. The credibility I have gained secures my seat at the table, and it's rightfully deserved. I would love to see you right there beside me.

I have either personally experienced these benefits through these two companies or seen them manifest in other places.

**-Recognition and Appointments:** Doors have opened to appointments, granting access to the opportunity to negotiate substantial contracts.

**- Level Up Positive Public Perception:** Recognition fosters a positive perception of your business within the community, enhancing its reputation as a reliable and reputable brand. Awards and quality marks can boost your business reputation, setting it apart from the crowd.

**- Social Impact:** These recognitions have enabled us to teach more people how to choose healthier lifestyles, saving them money on insurance bills, changing their medical experiences, and, in some cases, even saving lives.

**- Competitive Edge:** It is about setting your business apart from the rest. This competitive advantage distinguishes your business or organization from others in the market. They demonstrate that your business not only meets but often exceeds industry standards, setting a benchmark for excellence.

**-Grants:** The ability to qualify for big grants and secure the resources and tools to offer withing an amazing mentoring program for the women in our community.

**-Transforming Lives:** The lives of countless women in our community have been transformed creating a ripple effect that instigates lasting change across generations and puts a spotlight on gender and community biases.

**-Level Up Positive Public Perception:** Fosters a positive perception of your business within the community, enhancing its reputation as a reliable and reputable brand. Awards and quality marks can boost your business reputation, setting it apart from the crowd.

**-Boosts Bottom Line:** According to recent research published on Mindtools.com, Mind Tools Content Team titled *"The Benefits of Company Awards" stated an "award winning business can acquire a sales boost of 37% as well as 44% jump in their stock price."*

**This is how to leverage your certifications and awards.**

**Here you go!**

- Send out press releases to everyone on your email list, friends, family, peers.
- Post on all social media channels to announce your achievements, generating pride and excitement.
- Utilize email campaigns, social media, and your website to share your accomplishments, engaging both existing and potential customers.
- Feature on your website, prominently showcasing them on your website, marketing materials, and storefront.
- Celebrate with your team.
- Celebrate with the community.

Earning certifications and awards is not merely about recognition; it's a strategic investment in your business's growth and prosperity. These achievements elevate your credibility, set you apart from competitors, and establish you as a trusted community business leader. By effectively promoting your accolades, engaging with the community, and implementing targeted marketing strategies, you can attract more customers and foster long-term business success. Embrace your achievements, harness their power, and watch your small business thrive in today's competitive market.

These honors bestow upon you and your business or organization the trust and influence needed to effect substantial change. It's your moment to embark on this remarkable voyage.

# 11

## Back Matter

## SUPPORT HER JOURNEY:  C2 YOUR HEALTH WOMEN'S INITIATIVE EXPERIENCE

In the world of entrepreneurship, women often face unique challenges and barriers that hinder their growth and success. In this blog post, we'll explore how C2 Your Health Women's Initiative (C2YHWI) is making a significant impact by empowering women entrepreneurs and providing them with the support and resources they need to thrive.

C2YHWI was born out of a simple yet powerful idea: that women entrepreneurs should have access to mentors, resources, and a supportive community to help them succeed. The organization's founder, Cindy Cohen, RN, BS BA, understood firsthand the difficulties women face when pursuing their entrepreneurial dreams. Her own journey led her to create a non-profit organization dedicated to supporting and uplifting women in business.

### The Need for Support

Cindy's entrepreneurial journey began like many others. She sought information online, read books, attended seminars, and asked friends for advice. While these initial steps were helpful, she soon realized that finding women mentors and resources tailored to her needs was a challenge. This realization led her to a crucial insight: women entrepreneurs need a strong support system to thrive.

Statistics revealed a significant gender gap in entrepreneurship, especially in her home area of Saint Joseph County. Women comprised only 2% of business owners in the region, highlighting the need for more women to enter the world of entrepreneurship. The barriers women faced were numerous, including work-life balance, societal expectations, and a lack of confidence. Historically, women entrepreneurs experienced a higher failure rate compared to men, often due to a lack of role models, mentors, resources, and self-confidence.

## The Power of Mentoring

C2YHWI recognized the importance of mentorship in women's entrepreneurial success. A groundbreaking report revealed that 75% of women leaders found mentoring to be integral to their careers. Armed with this knowledge, C2YHWI set out to make a difference.

In 2018, C2YHWI expanded its mentoring program and became a nonprofit 501(c)(3) organization. The organization created mentoring fellowships and internships, addressing the most common obstacles faced by women entrepreneurs. The focus on health and wellness was deliberate, given the health crisis facing the nation. Chronic diseases and mental health issues were on the rise, making personal wellness an essential component of entrepreneurship.

## A Holistic Approach

C2YHWI's mission extended beyond mentoring. The organization organized women's business expo events, mentorship circles, symposiums, networking luncheons, and dinners. These events served as sources of business information, resources, and support, enabling women to succeed. The platform provided women micro-entrepreneurs with instant access to essential resources and education, eliminating barriers to entrepreneurship.

One of C2YHWI's signature initiatives is the Women's Entrepreneur Summit - Round Tables for Success. This summit offers valuable support for women entrepreneurs, providing mentorship, connecting them to vital resources, nurturing leadership skills, and boosting confidence. Health and wellness support are also integral components, recognizing the direct impact of personal health on business success.

## A Journey of Impact

Looking back on the journey, C2YHWI has made an impressive impact. The organization has connected with 974 remarkable local women, providing mentoring and support. Over 2,000 hours have been invested in direct mentoring, witnessing incredible growth and determination in these individuals.

Recognition has followed C2YHWI's efforts, with awards from Notre Dame University and Better World Books, acknowledging the organization's significant social impact. The mission to empower and uplift women in entrepreneurship has borne fruit, inspiring hope for a brighter future.

## Join the Mission

C2YHWI invites you to be a part of their mission to empower women in entrepreneurship. Your support can offer opportunities to aspiring girls and women, helping them achieve economic stability through entrepreneurship. By eliminating barriers and providing mentorship, you contribute to a more equitable and prosperous future for women in business.

To make a difference by making a donation to support C2YHWI's mission, go to www.supportherjourney.org.

Stay connected. Stay healthy. Stay you.

*"Individually, we are a drop of rain.*
*Together, we are an ocean.*
*With action, we are a title wave."*

*Cindy Cohen, Founder, President*
*C2 Your Health Women's Initiative Inc.*

INSPIRING BUSINESS
INSTITUTE

## ELEVATE YOUR BUSINESS:
## INSPIRING BUSINESS INSTITUTE

The dynamic team at Inspiring Business Institute LLC showcased their investment pitch and underwent thorough evaluations. A distinguished panel of judges, carefully selected by the McCloskey New Venture Competition staff, scrutinized 80 business concepts for their feasibility and potential as new ventures. This remarkable event took place at the Notre Dame University Idea Center - McCloskey New Venture Competition on April 21st, 2023, resulting in the well-deserved recognition of Inspiring Business Institute in Round 2.

Inspiring Business Institute is an innovative program designed to foster connections between city governments and organizations, offering vital support to small businesses. The program equips these businesses with the essential tools and connections required for accelerated growth, financial readiness, and community strengthening, thus contributing to the overall enhancement of the economic infrastructure.

The pilot program, aptly named the Mishawaka Business Institute, is set to commence in January 2024. This initiative is proudly supported by a collaboration between the City of Mishawaka, Inspire Mishawaka, Mishawaka Business Association, Wealth in Motion Consulting LLC, and C2 Your Health Women's Initiative Inc. It is dedicated to providing essential support to business owners residing or operating in Mishawaka.

We are excited to announce that the inaugural launch of IBI will take place through the City of Mishawaka via the Mishawaka Business Institute.

The esteemed members of the Inspiring Business Institute Competition Team are:

- Sonya Smith, Founder, CEO (with 29 years of experience **in** business and program development)

- Cindy Cohen, Founder, CEO (with 41 years of experience in mentoring, networking programs, and grant administration)

- Rick Williams, Director, City Administrator (Main Street America, grant Oakland County)

- Bryan Tanner, President, Administrator (Main Street America Grant, Non-profit)

- Mary Lou Stevens, Executive Director (Nonprofit business organizations)

- Keller Endler, Notre Dame Student (Major: Accounting, Class of 2026)

- Brooke Borton, Notre Dame Student (Major: Neuroscience & Behavior, Class of 2025)

To learn more about Inspiring Business Institute go to www.inspiringbusinessinstitute.com

Stay tuned for more updates on our inspiring journey!

JANUARY 2023                    INSPIRINGBUSINESSINSTITUTE.COM

**Inspiring Business Institute**

Inspiring the whole economic ecosystem, one city at a time

Inspiring Business Institute (IBI) develops an economic ecosystem bringing together city government, business associations, and chambers to provide a comprehensive certified platform for small business acceleration.

# Your success is our priority.
# Offering our program in your city means you will:

✓ Gain connections to our range of diverse suppliers

✓ Easily connect small businesses to local resources

✓ Develop your city's small business ecosystem

✓ Funding readiness small business

✓ Spark economic development which will

create jobs, increase wages, and increase local spending.

✓ Increase the tax base which will support schools, police,

infrastructure, and overall community development.

✓ Empower entrepreneurs who will generate more jobs

than any other sector of the economy

**Meet Our Team**

**Sonya Smith, EMBA, ACHE**
Wealth in Motion Consulting LLC
Owner
Experience: 29 Yrs. Business & Program
Development, Business Coaching

**Cindy Cohen RN, BS BA**
O2 Your Health Women's Initiative Inc
Founder, President
Experience: 41 Yrs. New Startup,
Business Development, Mentoring,
Networking Programing, Grant
Administration

**Let's improve our city's ecosystem, together.**

**Our program helps small businesses gain the connections and tools to accelerate, thereby strengthening the overall community & building up the economic infrastructure.**

## Inspiring Business Institute (IBI)

- 01 Needs Assessment (Survey)
- 02 Business Coaching Sessions (4)
- 03 Mentoring Sessions (4)
- 04 Business Resource Connections
- 05 Community Business Workshops
- 06 Business Excellence Certfication City Government Recognition
- 07 Community Recognition Awards

7 COMPONENTS BUSINESS SUCCESS IBI

**Step 1:** A business will fill out our comprehensive needs assessment.

**Step 2:** We'll develop a customized program including providing the necessary partnerships and resources for your city based on the assessment.

**Step 3:** We'll lead the program and assist businesses in implementing their learning materials.

BRYAN TANNER
ST. JOSEPH COUNTY
COUNCIL
★ ★ ★ ★ ★

"The social impact of Inspiring Business Institute is critical to local entrepreneurs, local businesses, that really are the driving force of small communities in our downtowns especially."

Inspiring Business Institute

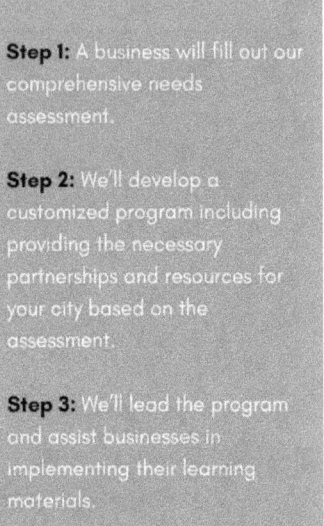

Business Coaching | Mentoring | Training | Certification

## Case Study: City of Mishawaka

inspiremishawaka.org/mbi

In our successful pilot program, we are working with the Mishawaka government to run the Mishawaka Business Institute through which we provide businesses with what they need to receive state and federal funds.

INSPIRINGBUSINESSINSTITUTE.COM

# Mishawaka Business Institute[31]

## What is Mishawaka Business Institute About?

Mishawaka Business Institute provides entrepreneurship and small business education, resources, networking, business coaching, business mentoring, and certification in partnership with the City of Mishawaka, Mishawaka Business Association, and Inspire Mishawaka.

## MBI Program Description

The program's goal is to introduce concepts, opportunities, and resources focused on business and industry specific goals and outcomes.

The program is comprised of three phases allowing each business to enter at current knowledge level.
- Phase I – Startups
- Phase II – Intermediate Business
- Phase III – Advanced

## Why is the Certification important with MBI?
- Recognition of specialized knowledge and skillsets

---

[31] Mishawaka Business Institute. Inspire Mishawaka.
www.inspiremishawaka.org and Mishawaka Business Association. Mishawaka Business Association – Mishawaka Indiana

- Demonstrates your commitment to superior professionalism, upholding industry standards and continued learning
- Gives you a competitive advantage
- Creates a solid foundation while boosting efficiencies
- Creates credibility by affiliation with the City, Mishawaka Business Association, and Inspire Mishawaka

**Ready to Get Started?**

Take the survey by clicking the button below to register your business. This is a great way to stay connected and in no way obligates you to the program. However, you will receive updates regarding business development, grants, services, and contracting opportunities by registering your Mishawaka business in our registry.

www.inspiremishawka.org

Program Administrators:
**Cindy Cohen, RN, BS BA+**
Founder, President
C2 Your Health Women's Initiative, Inc.
http://www.C2YHWI.org
cindycohenRN@yahoo.com

**Sonya Smith, EMBA, CAPM**
Founder, CEO
Wealth in Motion Consulting, LLC
www.wealthinmotion.net
sonya@wealthinmotion.net

# ACKNOWLEDGEMENTS

I'd like to express our heartfelt gratitude to the following individuals and organizations:

- We're honored to have received recognition and support from Notre Dame University's Idea Center, particularly through our participation as semifinalists in the McCloskey New Venture Competition and advancing to Round 2 in the Inspiring Business Institute competition.

- A huge thank you for the special recognition from Better World Books for choosing C2YHWI for the "Greatest Social Impact" award among new ventures featured at the McCloskey New Venture Competition. This funding supports the launch of Level Up Women Entrepreneur Residency program, and completion of the application process for the International Mentoring Association.

- A big thank you to 1st Source Bank for their invaluable support in empowering women entrepreneurs within our community through their involvement in the Women's Entrepreneur Summit and the Women Entrepreneur Excellence Program launch.

- I extend our deep appreciation to Traci Winston Williams, the visionary founder of H.O.T. Hear Our Tears, for collaborating with C2YHWI to establish the HOT DV Community Ambassador Program, which is making a significant impact.

- Our sincere thanks go to The Pokagon Fund for their belief in the potential of women from domestic violence environments seeking economic security. Their support has enabled us to take our mentoring program online, develop new curricula, provide education for women entrepreneurs starting their businesses and begin certification through the International Mentoring Association.

- A heartfelt thank you to the Mishawaka Business Association, Inspire Mishawaka, and the City of Mishawaka for supporting small businesses in Mishawaka with us.

-I would also like to extend our heartfelt gratitude to Sonya Smith, the owner of Wealth in Motion Consulting, for her exceptional partnership and dedication to our cause. Sonya's involvement in the McCloskey New Venture Competition, where we achieved Round 2, and her collaboration with the Inspiring Business Institute, have been instrumental in advancing our mission and providing invaluable opportunities for our organization. Thank you, Sonya, for your unwavering support and commitment to empowering women entrepreneurs and fostering their success. Your contributions are deeply appreciated.

-Special thanks to the visionary founders of the Women's Entrepreneur Summit and who have stood by my side for the last 6 years. Your unwavering belief, support, and dedication to our mission have been the driving force behind the positive transformation for women entrepreneurs in our community. Vida Harley, Debby Canarini, Traci Winston Williams, Ylonda Scott, and LaShonda Stewart.

- We are deeply grateful to Mayor Dave and the Common Council of Mishawaka, Mayor Mueller and the Common Council of South Bend, Mayor Rob Roberson of Elkhart, Mayor Gina Leichty and the City of Goshen, and Governor Eric Holcomb for acknowledging and honoring women entrepreneurs' contributions and for proclaiming November 19th as part of the global celebration of Women's Entrepreneurship Day. Your support means the world to us and the women we serve. Thank you!

## CONTRIBUTORS

Debby Canarini
Debby Canarini, Mindset Coach
www.DebbyCannarini.com
Knox, IN

LaChelle Barnet, CEO
Owner, Pivot Your Brand
www.theresetroom.com
South Bend, IN

Laquisha Jackson
Owner, Soulful Kitchen LLC
Founder, Hope For The Hungry Inc.
www.soulfulkitchensb.com
South Bend, IN

LaQuita Hughes
Founder, T&T Ministries, Inc. (501c3)
Facebook Group: Testimony & Tea Ministries, Inc.
Owner, Angels of Integrity Youth & Family Services, LLC
Owner, Milestone Academy, LLC
http://bit.ly/milestoneacademy
South Bend, IN

Maria Flemming (Tanksley)
Owner, Senior Resource Network
www.Seniorresourcenetwork.org
South Bend, IN

Nontuthuzelo Sisale
Mandela Washington Alumna 2023
LinkedIN: Nontuthuzelo Sisale
Bulawayo Province, Zimbabwe

Nyauhango Wakwa Kaunga
Kate's Kitchen
Facebook: Nyauhango Wakwa Kaunga
South Bend, IN - Malawi, Africa

Sonya Smith, CEO
Owner, Wealth in Motion Consulting LLC
www.wealthinmotion.net
C-founder, Inspiring Business Institute - Cofounder
www.inspiringbusinessinstitute.com
South Bend, IN

Stacey Oberly Black
Michiana Women Rise
Facebook: Michiana Women Rise
Elkhart / Goshen, IN

Stacey Wing
Senior Retail Business Banker
1st Source Bank
www.1stsource.com
South Bend, IN

Stephanie Thomas
AVP, SBA Relationship Officer – TORCH
First Savings Bank – Small Business Lending
www.fsb-sbl.com
South Bend, IN

Tina Shalane MMS, Business Consultant
www.tinashalne.com
247mmblc.newzenler.com
Fort Wayne, IN

Tomecia Tillman
JJT Dispatch & Logistics
Facebook: JJT Dispatch & Logistics
South Bend, IN

Traci Winston
Founder, H.O.T. Hear Our Tears
www.hearourtears.com
Owner Unique Boutique International LLC
www.uniqueboutique547.com
South Bend, IN

Vida Harley
Founder, Women Entrepreneurs Matter
On Facebook: Women Entrepreneurs Matter
South Bend, IN

Ylonda Scott
Ylonda Scott, CEO-Personal & Business Development Coach
Owner, SheBoss Oasis Retreats & Conferences
www.shebossoasisretreats.info
Niles, MI


**BUSINESS PROFILE:**
**C2 Your Health Women's Initiative Inc. (501c3)**

### Overview

C2 Your Health Women's Initiative is a pioneering organization committed to the empowerment and well-being of women entrepreneurs. Our mission is to provide women from diverse backgrounds with the tools, resources, and mentorship needed to excel in their entrepreneurial journeys. We firmly believe that when women succeed, communities thrive, and our organization is dedicated to fostering economic security, personal growth, and business success for women in our community.

## Key Initiatives and Programs

Women Entrepreneur Excellence Program:
A comprehensive program offering mentorship, training, and resources to help women entrepreneurs start and grow their businesses.

Online / Offline Mentoring Program:
We offer an online mentoring platform to connect experienced entrepreneurs with those in need of guidance and support.

H.O.T. DV Community Ambassador Program:
In partnership with C2YHWI, H.O.T. Hear Our Tears, and The Pokagon Fund through the *Women Move Forward Initiative* we support survivors of domestic violence by providing mentorship and resources to help them achieve economic independence.

Educational Partnerships:
Collaborations with colleges, universities, and business institutions to provide women entrepreneurs with access to business competitions, funding opportunities, and educational resources.

Community Connections:
*Hey Women Entrepreneurs Let's Meetup*! Through monthly networking meetups and workshops, we connect women in the community to mentoring, role models, leadership, business strategies and leadership development. We support connections and encourage participation in the chamber of commerce, business organizations that support entrepreneur business development on the local and state level. *Women Entrepreneur (WE) Ambassador Project* is assembling an elite trail blazing group of women to kick-start this amazing project designed to uplift and empower women entrepreneurs while providing important resource connections, guidance, support, and the community leadership women entrepreneurs need to thrive.

Annual Women's Conference:
Each November, during Entrepreneur Week, the *Women's Entrepreneur Summit - Round Tables for Success* hosts a 7-hour conference that brings together women entrepreneurs from diverse backgrounds. Our aim is to connect and empower women by providing role models, mentoring, resources, and confidence-boosting activities. The event features inspirational women entrepreneurs, panel discussions with Q&A sessions, roundtable discussions, and a networking lunch. Topics include scaling-up, innovation, and effective business strategies, all shared through the inspiring stories of remarkable women in our community. This is where current and aspiring women entrepreneurs gain insights, tips, and inspiration to achieve their goals while balancing personal commitments. Be the best version of yourself and reach your aspirations with the support of your peers.

Leadership:
Our organization is led a Board of Directors, a Community Advisory Board, by a dedicated team of women entrepreneurs, professionals who are passionate about promoting women's entrepreneurship and empowerment.

Women Entrepreneur Recognition:
We    proudly acknowledge and celebrates the remarkable contributions of women entrepreneurs in our community. We honor their achievements in multiple ways, including the annual *Women-Owned Business Top 10* in partnership with Ylonda Scott of Ylonda's Empowering Women Business Retreat Agency. Additionally, we recognize exceptional culinary talent at the Taste of *Michiana Women Entrepreneur Chef Competition* with the prestigious *Best Bites Award*. At the *Women Entrepreneur Summit*, we applaud outstanding charity efforts, and at the *Expo for Women*, we recognize our organization as the *Outstanding Charity of the Year* and at the *Women's Showcase Event*, we recognize *Michiana Woman Entrepreneur To Watch of the Year*.

Inspiring Business Institute / Mishawaka Business Institute:
Cindy Cohen partnership with Co-founder with Sonya Smith, Co-founder, providing entrepreneur support for all genders, ethnic groups, and socioeconomic backgrounds through city, business, and organizations focused on providing entrepreneurial and small business support through business coaching, business mentoring, workshops, and resource connections.

At *C2 Your Health Women's Initiative*, we are committed to fostering a thriving community of women entrepreneurs, breaking down barriers, and helping women achieve their business dreams. Join us in our mission to create a more inclusive and prosperous future for all women in business. www.C2YHWI.org #C2YHWI

## ADDITIONAL C2YHWI RESOURCES

Women Move Forward Mentoring Community - Free online classes, and Women Entrepreneur Excellence mentoring, course, and certification. www.womenmoveforward.info

H.O.T. Domestic Violence Community Ambassador Program
www.womenmoveforward.com

Mental Health Toolbox with FREE App
www.womenmoveforward.info

C2YHWI Women Entrepreneur Happenings
www.womenmoveforwardsignup.com

C2YHWI Donation Center
www.SupportHerJourney.org

Women Entrepreneur Happenings Email List
www.entrepreneurwomen.online

Women Entrepreneur Excellence preapplication interview
www.womenmoveforwardsignup.com

Cindy's List Directory Women Entrepreneurs, Women-owned
Business Enterprises
Facebook Group: Cindys List

## AUTHOR'S ONLINE PRESENCE

Cindy Cohen RN, BS BA
Owner, C2 Your Health LLC
Founder, President, C2 Your Health Women's Initiative Inc.
501(c)(3)
Email: CindyCohenRN@yahoo.com

Follow C2YHWI:
Facebook: http://www.Facebook.com/C2YHWI
Facebook Groups:
- www.facebook.com/groups/womenmoveforward,
- www.facebook.com/womenentrepreneurexcellence

Platform: Mentoring Community www.womenmoveforward.info

Instagram: http://www.instagram.com/cindycohenrn

Follow Cindy Cohen RN
- Facebook: http://www.Facebook.com/CindyCohenRN
- Twitter: http://www.twitter.com/cindycohen
- LinkedIn: http://www.linkedin.com/in/cindycohenrn
- Instagram: http://www.instagram.com/cindycohenrn
- Professional: http://about.me/cindycohenRN

Find C2 Your Health LLC
- Website: www.cindycohenrn.com
- Facebook: www.facebook.com/c2yourhealth

Visit Inspiring Business Institute / Mishawaka Business Institute -www.inspiringbusinessinstitute.com www.inspiremishawaka.com

Donate: Your donations are tax deductible as designated by the IRS. www.supportherjourney.org

## LIST OF WORKS

### Books

- 2023 She Means Business: Breaking Through and Scaling Up published KDP publishing
- 2023 Selfcare Planner eBook published on C2YHWI Mentoring Community
- 2021 Woman Entrepreneur Small Business Startup Guide Think Business Basics, Amazon Publishing
- 2020 Super Charge Your Body Step by Step Guide to Boosting Your Immunity eBook publishing
- 2015 Transform 365 Today Program Guide / Weight Loss, Amazon Publishing
- 2014 What's on Your Plate A Simple Guide to Healthy Cooking, Second Edition, Amazon Publishing
- 2013 What's on Your Plate A Simple Guide to Healthy Cooking, Amazon Publishing
- 2013 AHA BetterU special edition 2nd edition June
- 2013 AHA Launch Copy, 2nd edition January
- 2012 Prevention Benefits Healthy Employees Cost More, Amazon Publishing
- 2012 Self Marketing Handbook Women's Guide to Marketing Online and Offline, LORD Publishing (2nd publishing, 3rd edition January 2013
- 2011 Self Marketing Handbook Women's Guide to Marketing Online and Offline, LORD Publishing (1st publishing)

- 2010 7 Nuts and Bolts in Your Networking Tool Box, Amazon Publishing
- 2010 Expert Guide to Small Business Success (Chapter – "Face to Face),  Expert Publishing
- 2005 Generation to Generation Cookbook, Morris Press
- 2000 Noodles to Strudels, Morris Press

## Magazines

- 2023 Small Business Showcase
- 2018 Wellness Wednesday
- 2016 KIT Indy
- 2016 Fresh Lifestyle
- 2015 - 2016 Michiana Life
- 2013 - 2016 Small Biz Forward
- 2010 - 2012  Ezine Expert Author
- 2010 - 2011  Exhilarated Living Magazine (this is now out of print however here is November Issue Online.

## Blogs

- Support Her Journey: C2 Your Health Women's Initiative Experience
- Women Entrepreneur Pajama Party Interviews
- Nutz 4 Nutrition
- WOW Networking
- Prevention Benefits Work
- BetterU – Michiana American Heart Association

## ABOUT THE AUTHOR:

For nearly three decades, Cindy Cohen has been a trailblazing force in the realm of health and wellness entrepreneurship. With a remarkable journey that began in 1991, she has dedicated herself to transforming lives, empowering communities, and leaving a lasting legacy of positive change. Cindy's unwavering commitment to making a difference culminated in the creation of C2 Your Health Women's Initiative Inc., a nonprofit organization that has become a beacon of hope and empowerment for women in underserved communities.

Cindy Cohen's visionary spirit has been the driving force behind the success of C2 Your Health Women's Initiative Inc. Drawing from over 28 years of entrepreneurial experience in the health and wellness sector, Cindy possesses a unique blend of compassion and business acumen. Her innovative approach to addressing the complex challenges faced by women in low-income neighborhoods and domestic violence situations has ignited a transformative movement, inspiring women to dream big and nurture next-step thinking.

Come join us and countless other women who have dared to defy convention, break through barriers, and scale up their businesses. Together, we'll rewrite the narrative and create a world where every woman truly means business.

"Climbing the ladder of success, she broke through barriers and scaled new heights, proving that in business, determination is the key to her empire's flight."

Cindy Cohen RN, BS BA, Founder, President
C2 Your Health Women's Initiative Inc.

www.ingramcontent.com/pod-product-compliance
Lightning Source LLC
Chambersburg PA
CBHW072359290526
45794CB00001B/119